A Greening of
Imaginations

A Greening of Imaginations

Walking the Songlines of Holy Scripture

Herbert O'Driscoll

CHURCH
PUBLISHING
INCORPORATED

Church Publishing
19 East 34th Street
New York, NY 10016
www.churchpublishing.org

Cover design by Jennifer Kopec, 2Pug Design
Interior design and typesetting by Beth Oberholtzer

Library of Congress Cataloging-in-Publication Data

Names: O'Driscoll, Herbert, author.
Title: A greening of imaginations : walking the songlines of Holy Scripture / Herbert O'Driscoll.
Description: New York : Church Publishing, 2019. | Includes index.
Identifiers: LCCN 2018039116 (print) | LCCN 2018048411 (ebook) | ISBN 9781640651456 (ebook) | ISBN 9781640651449 (pbk.)
Subjects: LCSH: Bible. New Testament—Criticism, interpretation, etc. | Storytelling—Religious aspects—Christianity.
Classification: LCC BS2361.3 (ebook) | LCC BS2361.3 .O37 2019 (print) | DDC
   252/.03—dc23
LC record available at https://lccn.loc.gov/2018039116

*For Paula, and for the wonderful people
in our lives who once were our children.*

There is another song I think about. "I love to tell the story.". . . If western history has proved one thing, it is that the narratives of the Bible are essentially inexhaustible. The Bible is terse, the gospels are brief, and the result is that every moment and every detail merits pondering and can always appear in a richer light. The Bible is about human beings, human families—in comparison with other ancient literatures the realism of the Bible is utterly remarkable—so we can bring our own feelings to bear in the reading of it. In fact, we cannot do otherwise, if we know the old, old story well enough to give it a life in our thoughts.

Marilynne Robinson, "Wondrous Love"
in *When I Was a Child I Read Books*, 126.

Contents

Part IV: Letters Lost and Newly Found

Prologue
Early morning July 1937

I was nine years old and spending my school holidays on my grandfather's farm in the Townsland of Donaguile in the County of Kilkenny in Ireland.

About a quarter of a mile along the country road from the driveway gate of our farm, there was a thatched cottage. Three people lived there, two sisters and a brother. They were all, if memory serves, in their late fifties, though this would have been further along in the cycle of life than it is today.

One day I was sent over to the cottage to buy some eggs. Jim Brennan brought them out to me and I duly handed over the money I had been given. For the first time, I noticed something about Jim. I could see how hesitantly he walked, how weak and light his voice was, and how hollow-chested he had become. I was too young to realize that I was looking at the ravages of tuberculosis, a scourge that affected something like 40 percent of the population of rural Ireland in those long ago 1930s.

But something happened as I stood in front of Jim. Having become aware of his fragility, the fact that he lived in this cottage with his two sisters, Mary and Lizzie, struck me with an utterly new significance that was both thrilling and frightening. Suddenly in a child's mind two households merged—one was this cottage where I stood, the other a home in the pages of the Gospel according to John.

On one of the few journeys Jesus took to Jerusalem, he came to the village of Bethany. It was here that he met a woman named Martha who offered him and his friends hospitality.

This small house, where Martha lived with her sister Mary and their brother Lazarus, would come to be the one home where Jesus would feel deeply welcome. This is where, on another occasion, he would spend what would be his last hours of freedom before entering the city, sharing supper with his friends, being arrested, tried, and executed.

John writes, however, of something that happened before that—a mysterious, even terrifying event when Jesus raised Lazarus from the dead. To me, and indeed to all Church of Ireland children of my generation, this story from the pages of the gospel writer would have been as familiar as any other part of our education.

It was therefore quite natural that while I was walking very slowly homeward, as small boys are apt to do, I thought about all this. I remembered reading that Lazarus had died and that Jesus had called him back to life. I began to wonder about Jim Brennan and his sisters. After all, this household next door to our farm was a mirror image of that long-ago home in Bethany. In both houses there lived a brother with two sisters. In both families the brother had become ill. Could it be true then that Jim had died and been mysteriously called back to life? Was there some corner of the cottage property where I might find a dark and hidden place with a stone guarding its entrance? The very thought of this was at the same time both fascinating and fearful. I have no memory of mentioning these thoughts when I reached home.

Looking back across many years at that small boy returning to the farm with the newly purchased eggs, I realize now that he had just experienced what would become two lasting elements of his life flowing together. One was the world of Holy Scripture and the other was the gift of imagination.

Some years later, when I was thirteen, I went to boarding school. In those days the Church of Ireland set an annual examination in religion for all students in its schools. As the time for the actual examination would approach, all other subjects in the school's daily schedule were cancelled. From 9:00 a.m. to 3:00 p.m.—with of course breaks for mid-morning and lunch—we studied Old Testament, New Testament, and Church Catechism. This would continue for at least two weeks.

Naturally at that stage of our lives, the narrative passages of the Bible were especially fascinating. For me, and I am by no means alone in this, those narratives have never left. In fact, they have continued to intrigue and fascinate me all my life.

I realize now that scripture was offered to us in a very natural and uncritical way. Looking back, I think it was understood that we would grow into other ways of finding truths in the stories, not by rejecting our first understandings but rather by having them deepened. This has certainly been my experience.

The second element that has always been part of my life is that of imagination. Works of literary imagination I find irresistible, whether they be classical myths, stories of quest, journeys to unknown lands, or travels in time. I have always been drawn to such tales.

There came a day in Calgary, Alberta when a conversation brought those two elements of my life together. I was rector of a parish in the city, and I got to know a local rabbi named Peter. He was a few years younger than I. We were talking one morning about the very ancient world of Jewish Midrash. I had long been aware of this rich tradition in which rabbis would enter into a biblical story to explore endless facets of the story that could be used for teaching about human experience. At some stage in our conversation, Peter remarked that in contrast to Jewish reflection on scripture, much Christian preaching tends to regard the text as being all there is to work with. The Jewish approach to scripture probes the text for ever more levels of meaning and application.

I recall that I had two reactions. The first was realizing that I had instinctively been doing something like this in my teaching and preaching; the second was feeling immensely encouraged that I had the good company of the long tradition of Judaism. There was a third reaction—a determination to develop this skill as much as I could in the way that I explored scripture from then on.

Among the many results of that morning are these pages, a small collection of biblical passages where I do what I simply love doing: applying my imagination to various moments in the Bible, asking myself questions. What would it have been like to be there at that moment? What were those men and women feeling then? Why did they act and react as they did? Such questions abound and draw one deeper and deeper into the text.

Come back with me to childhood—to the moment when my imagination made a link between the cottage in Donaguile in which Mary and Lizzie and Jim Brennan lived and the house in Bethany where Lazarus lived with his two sisters, Mary and Martha. For me, my lifelong relationship to that moment is rather like hearing a wonderful piece of music when one is very young and hearing it again in mature years. It is of course the same music, but it speaks on many more levels than it did in childhood.

"When I was a child," wrote Paul to the community at Corinth, "I spoke like a child, I thought like a child, I reasoned like a child. When I became an adult, I put an end to childish ways" (1 Cor. 12:11). The only way in which I would dare to correct the great apostle is to suggest humbly that perhaps life is not so much a putting away of childish things as it is to experience their maturing in wonderful ways.

I would like to offer you these reflections on Holy Scripture, not merely that you read how the text has fed my imagination, but to allow your own imagination to go voyaging down the songlines of Holy Scripture.

Victoria, British Columbia, Canada
All Saintstide 2018

PART I

Our Lord's Childhood

CHAPTER 1

Annunciation

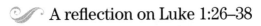 A reflection on Luke 1:26–38

Within each of us there is a country, its landscapes as varied as the outer landscapes we travel, sometimes haunting and captivating, sometimes barren and forbidding.

As with the landscapes of outer geography, so it is with our inner life; there is always more to be explored. We ourselves may be the explorer or it may be someone else who wishes to know us intimately because they love us or perhaps because we have sought their guidance. In fact, if our relationships are to remain healthy, our mutual exploring must never end, and every discovery is prelude to another.

The village girl in our story is young. We are told nothing else about her at the moment we meet her in scripture. Later, we will see that this young woman had a remarkable capacity to remain faithful under great stress.

We know too that she was visited by an angel. There is nothing unusual in this. Since angels are the messengers of God sent to offer direction for our lives, all of us have been visited by an angel, most often quite unknowingly. Sometimes we have ignored their calling and gone our own way.

At other times we have heard and obeyed, setting off in the direction in which we have been pointed, doing the tasks for which we are fitted, and living the fulfilled lives God has in store for us.

Luke names the angel who comes on this mission. Perhaps this is to point out that this is not just any angel but one of the greatest of them, Gabriel, who is nothing less than an archangel. By naming the great messenger, the evangelist is almost certainly implying that this particular angelic mission is of surpassing significance.

If a friend had asked this young woman about the moment when she felt visited, she might have said only that she had received a message. She might have tried to describe how she felt fear in the first moments of becoming aware of a presence, how that fear passed, how she felt strangely reassured, and how she then knew that she would give birth. I would think it almost certain that she would have told these things to her husband Joseph. Perhaps years later she told them to her son in some moment of intimacy.

About the months of her pregnancy we know almost nothing. We have to assume that it went normally. However, we know also that those months were not always untroubled. For instance, at an early stage in her pregnancy she felt impelled to make a dangerous journey to see her cousin Elizabeth, an older relative who was also pregnant. Then toward the end of those months, when she was very near her time, she found herself having to make a longer and more dangerous journey at the demand of the Roman authorities occupying her country. We know that she came to a crowded town and that she and her husband Joseph were directed to a hillside cave which was used as a stable. There, amid their few belongings, she gave birth to her child.

The business of an angel, like the one who came to Mary and—let us not forget—also to Joseph, is to point us to further exploration within ourselves. Because they come from God, angels know how much in us has been brought to realization and how much is still waiting to be explored. The angel knows and can help us to discover what gifts given to us at birth have never yet been used. When they come to us, these messengers of God ask us to give birth within ourselves in some way. They may ask us to give birth to a work of art, or to a new relationship, or to a time of self-discovery. As we live those experiences we may learn, sometimes with great astonishment, that we are capable of things far beyond our imagining, whether it be bearing a great burden, serving in a great cause, facing a daunting crisis, or nourishing another life.

Whatever we are called to do or to be, we will find this young woman Mary's experience speaking to our lives.

When, led by some angelic visitation, we explore and give birth to new possibilities within us, then we find meaning and vocation in our lives.

We call this young woman blessed because her willingness to give birth to her promised child became a blessing to the whole world. We also call her blessed because she and her child Jesus who has become our Lord and Savior have become a blessing to us. The gift of life that she gave to her son is prelude to the gift of life he gives to us.

CHAPTER 2

The Guardian

A reflection on Matthew 1:18–25

I have always felt that when Jesus suggested to his follow-
ers that they relate to God in terms of a loving father, he
was doing so because of his own loving relationship with
the man whom he would have regarded as father, particu-
larly in the early years of childhood.

I also feel that the best way to meet Joseph is to try to
grasp what it might have meant for him to wrestle with an
experience that must have been shattering. I imagine him
trying to come to terms with what the woman he loved has
just told him. I think it likely that the hour is late at night,
perhaps not long before dawn, a time when we often wrestle
with troubled thoughts, and when we sometimes dream . . .

In desperation he tried to force himself to think clearly.
There were only two things of which he could be certain.
The woman to whom he was publicly betrothed was by
her own word pregnant. At the same time he was only too
aware that he himself was not the father of the unborn child.

Certain courses of action were open to him. One was
to divorce as quickly and as quietly as possible. He had

absolutely no wish to bring shame on anyone, least of all the woman for whom he had deep affection, as well as deep respect for her family. Again and again he searched for some other course of action that might help. Exhausted and miserable, he slipped into a troubled and restless sleep.

Years later, whenever he thought about that night—and he would remember it for the rest of his life, particularly when he would look at the growing boy who worked with him at the bench—he could never be sure whether the encounter had been dreamt or experienced in some mysterious reality beyond normal experience. The figure that addressed him was majestic, yet neither fearsome nor threatening. He had felt cared for and valued. Even such words would always be insufficient to describe the encounter.

He knew immediately that the figure was an angel. All his life since childhood he had been told of such visitations. What was disturbing and astounding was that he should be the recipient of such an encounter.

The voice was rich beyond description, gentle and reassuring. The very first word was his own name, spoken in a way that utterly affirmed and respected him. "Joseph, son of David, do not be afraid." Only in that moment did he recall that Mary, speaking of her own encounter, had likewise been assured that there was no need to fear. The voice continued. "Do not be afraid to take Mary as your wife, for the child conceived in her is from the Holy Spirit. She will bear a son."

He realized that he had no idea of the meaning of what was being said to him but for some reason it didn't seem to matter. He felt himself to be in a state of utter trust. Things would be as this voice said they would be, no less, no more. So securely was he held within the aura of the visitor that he took a moment to realize that the voice had taken on a commanding tone. "You are to name him Jesus," he was told. The tone was quiet but it allowed no question nor did it accept failure to respond.

Suddenly he knew why the messenger had come. Suddenly he realized the one thing that in his fear and confusion he had been withholding—his acceptance of the child that lay in Mary's womb. That acceptance, freely given, was the one thing needed to make this boy not only Mary's son but his too. Now he knew the reason for the immense gift of this visit. He had been given this gift to show him that there was a gift he had to give to this unborn child. His life was now for only one purpose—to bring up the boy, to treasure him, and to love him for whatever years lay ahead.

Tears welled up in Joseph as he felt acceptance and gratitude flood over him. The angelic aura began to dim until it was no longer present. As it faded, the first rays of the morning sun splashed across the walls of the simple workshop in which he slept.

From now on, he thought, there would have to be a home, however simple, a home for his wife and for the boy. Who knows, he might yet make a good carpenter of him. Tears welled again, but this time they were tears of joy.

CHAPTER 3

The Star

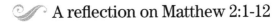 A reflection on Matthew 2:1-12

When distinguished figures from a remote foreign power arrived in a regime ruled by a paranoid despot, there was immediate suspicion. This suspicion was made even more potent when the strangers offered astronomical and astrological evidence for the birth of a child who could become a possible threat to the despot. A memory of the experience recalled by one of the visitors in later years . . .

The compound where he worked before retirement was situated atop a high mountain ridge in the western part of the kingdom. In the distance on a clear day, one could see the great gulf that is fed from the north by the Tigris and the Euphrates. Beyond the gulf to the west, the vast desert stretches to the edge of Egypt. For centuries Egypt had been their enemy.

The view most significant for his work had always been that of the night skies. As scientists, he and his two colleagues studied the constellations, then consulted the tables and records kept over the centuries. They assigned meaning to their movements and reported to the palace authorities. They reported to the king.

The memory that would stay forever in his mind began with a report that two of the greatest planets, Saturn and Jupiter, seemed to be converging in the constellation we call Pisces or "the Fish." Their light began to grow brighter until they came to dominate the heavens, so much so that after consulting with their senior staff, a report was made to the palace.

As he recalled, it had an immediate response. Among their observations was the fact that the convergence seemed to be moving in a westerly direction. Orders came to them to select a small group of their staff to travel westward, in order to continue studying the phenomenon. They would be given an escort. Their route would take them north along the east bank of the Euphrates. At a certain point, they would cross the river to join the Roman highway system at Dura Europos, the most Eastern outpost and garrison of the Roman Empire. There the escort would leave them. From there on, they would have to make their own decisions.

They had very specific orders. They were to look for any signs of political or military disturbance on the eastern edge of the Roman Empire or in the vicinity of Egypt, both of which could be a threat to imperial interests in Persia. In case they might find themselves in any diplomatic encounters, they were directed to take with them some symbolic and exotic gifts that would suitably impress their hosts. The memory he treasured all his life was not the journey, but its destination.

All went well until they arrived in southern Palestine. Its puppet king retained power only with the support of the Roman occupiers. By the time the three paid their respects to him, they knew that the regime was utterly corrupt and cordially hated by the local people.

He remembered night falling as they left Herod. At the end of the great circular driveway that led to Herod's fortress, they found a young man who approached them saying that someone wished to meet with the three visitors, and that he would guide them to the rendezvous. It was a very difficult decision to make, because he knew that it could well be a trap. He questioned the youth carefully before deciding to accept the invitation.

He remembered that they approached a small village under a starlit sky. He estimated they were now about four miles from Herod's fortress. To his knowledge, they were not being followed.

The house that welcomed them was that of the village rabbi. After the customary gestures of welcome and an offer of refreshment, which the three accepted, the rabbi introduced his wife and told them that their guide had been his son.

When they had partaken of a simple but delicious meal, the host gestured them to follow the family to the back of the house. They watched in astonishment as he removed a section of the earthen floor and beckoned them down a simple ladder. A whole living area had been hollowed out and furnished. A young woman sat holding a child. He would estimate the child to be about two years old. Her husband stood behind them, he somewhat older than she.

He didn't know why or how, but suddenly he knew with absolute certainty that they had found what they had come for. He also knew that they had not discovered what their political masters had sent them here to find. Instead, he had an overpowering conviction that a higher power had directed them to something infinitely more significant.

He had been at the shrines of countless gods, both those of their own Persian empire and those of Rome, but nothing had ever addressed him with the power of that moment. All he could say is that in the presence of an ineffable majesty, they found themselves on their knees.

It was Melchior who remembered the gifts. They still had them in their baggage, because they had encountered no powerful ruler worthy of them. Here in this lamplit room with its earthen walls, they could only hope that these gifts would be found worthy of this child. When they had presented the gifts, the rabbi beckoned them to leave.

It was the rabbi who told them everything. They found that he shared with them the common commercial language of the east, Aramaic. Quietly he told them of the boy's birth, how the skies had sung. They told him of their sightings among the planets. He was not surprised. He told them too of the great fear of Herod's death squads. For two years he and many others had protected the child, moving the family from house to house, sometimes hiding them in the vast cave system in the walls of the escarpment near the village. They asked him the name of the place. He replied that the village was called Bethlehem. Since time immemorial the name meant "House of Bread."

At that point, the rabbi's voice became anxious. He feared that time was running out. Herod's fear and paranoia made him persistent. The family needed to get away. At this point he asked for the three visitors' help. He felt their coming had been providential. Would they at least escort the refugees to the border with Egypt?

There was never a moment's doubt. Preparations had already been made for such an opportunity as this. Long before dawn, they had moved away from the vast bulk of Herod's fortress and were heading west for the coastal road—the Way of the Sea. From the Egyptian border, when farewells had been said, they would eventually turn east toward the Dead Sea, then north on the other great road— the Way of the Kings—pursuing their long journey home.

At some point on that return trip, they agreed on their report. They had found no kings plotting against Persia, no armies marching from Egypt, no military maneuvers along the Roman border. Only the three colleagues would ever know that a king greater than all kings was now growing to manhood on the earth.

CHAPTER 4

Flight for Survival

A reflection on Luke 2:22–40
and Matthew 2:13–23

*Jerusalem—a cold February afternoon in 1993. I am
standing at the railings that bar entry to the ruined steps
at the south end of the temple area. Behind me, the afternoon Jerusalem traffic is heavy and noisy, the swirling air
filled with dust and fumes. I am aware that centuries ago,
a young couple brought their child to the bottom of these
steps, joining the never-ending flood of pilgrims.*

*If a long persistent tradition is true, the parents of the
young woman carrying her child had their home somewhere on the long slope that falls away behind me into the
Kidron Valley. Their daughter Mary, with her husband
Joseph, would have slept in that home the night before
this obligation to take their newborn to the temple to be
dedicated to God.*

*But I have questions as I stand here. I am trying to
reconcile two gospel records, those of Luke and Matthew.
My questions all boil down to one: when did our Lord's*

parents, realizing that they might well become the focus of Herod's paranoia, decide to flee the Bethlehem area? Matthew tells me of that flight. Luke tells me of the child's dedication here in Jerusalem . . .

Ever since the exotic and rather overpowering visitors had arrived in Bethlehem, obviously interested in their newborn son for reasons they could not even guess at, both parents had felt uneasy. The society ruled by Herod was one of fear, secret police, and paid informers. Safety lay in remaining anonymous.

From this village, where they had sought temporary lodging while visiting the south for the recent Roman census, he could see the vast mountain fortress used by Herod as both residence and military headquarters. It loomed above them only four kilometers away. Its troops were constantly around the village; some of the senior officers' families were quartered in its better houses.

Everything in Joseph made him anxious to return to the Galilee as quickly as possible. The child had already been circumcised by the local rabbi. One thing more remained: to take him to the temple in Jerusalem for his dedication. Joseph had been postponing this to allow Mary to rest after giving birth.

A casual conversation over a drink with one of the workers from the Herodium changed everything. Apparently, some exotic foreign visitors had requested an audience with Herod. They had asked questions about an ancient prophecy concerning a child of destiny who might be born somewhere in the area. His interlocutor was vague about the details, but Joseph could hardly wait for their chat to end before rushing back to the family's makeshift lodging and telling Mary. To his relief, she immediately understood and agreed. They should leave.

Hurriedly collecting their few possessions, they slipped away in the predawn hours. They had decided to go north to the Jerusalem area. It was large, bustling with people from all over the empire, and it was the home of Mary's parents. There they could think through their next decision.

Reaching the house in Jerusalem, they were given the loving welcome and warm hospitality that Mary needed. Joseph could see her relax in a way he hadn't known since they had left Nazareth. That evening, the hope was expressed that they could stay for at least a few days before setting off for the north and home. Meanwhile, there was the matter of their son's dedication. It was agreed they would go to the temple on the morrow.

The moment they set foot on the first of the giant stone steps, they felt taken by the crowd and swept through the entrance into the vast court of the Gentiles. Joseph particularly, used to his village life, had no prior experience of this pandemonium on every side of them.

From earlier visits to the temple, Mary was able to point out the area where he could see booths selling the birds and animals that were necessary for making the required sacrifices. Leaving Mary and the babe in the shelter of one of the entrance arches, Joseph went to buy the two birds they needed. It was the cheapest purchase possible.

He had just paid his money and was turning to go back when he overheard the word "Bethlehem." His instinct was to swing around to identify the source of the voice. Just in time, some inner sense warned him not to show curiosity. Pretending to inspect a nearby booth he listened, trying to follow the voice in the hubbub of voices on every side. He heard more words: "Herod," . . . "house searches," . . . then he heard the dread word *"children,"* and suddenly, everything changed. He listened, appalled and sickened at what he was hearing. Every male child under two! Joseph had always known, as did most people, the murderous acts done by Herod over the years, but this was beyond comprehension. He realized with chilling clarity how near their child had come to being slaughtered.

He became aware of the two birds hanging on his belt, and of the fact that someone was anxiously waiting for him to return. As he worked his way back to where he had left his wife and child, he made two decisions he would never regret. He would not mention the terror they had narrowly escaped, and even though he was deeply concerned for their security, he would not insist that they leave immediately without carrying out the dedication for which they had come. It was all important that this day remain a joyful memory.

Some hours later they would leave the temple area, their son duly dedicated to God. They would thankfully move out of the press of people and the shouting of half-heard conversations, coming down the great steps and heading for the house.

Many times in the future they would think back on the joys of that day, even though they would also vividly remember its ending and its searing decisions that had to be made before nightfall. Mary would recall details she obviously cherished: the moment of dedication when the priest handed back her child, the high tremulous songs of the elderly Simeon and Anna, the amazing dreams these old people seemed to have for her babe's future. Joseph would listen to her, realizing that he himself had moved through the ceremony in a state of numbness, still reacting to the obscenity perpetrated in Bethlehem, forcing himself to seem part of what was taking place around them in the ceremony. He would also give silent thanks for his decision not to share the terrible things overheard in that long-ago temple crowd, and not to insist that they leave the area immediately without completing the ceremony.

Not until she had slept did he come to her with the news he had kept to himself. As she listened, he could see that she fully understood that they could not now return to Nazareth. It was simply too dangerous. They would still be within the jurisdiction of the Herodian family power network. He knew the depth of her disappointment, because he shared it. He couldn't help admiring her composure as she laid the child down to sleep so that she could prepare for leaving. They both told her parents, thanking them but explaining why they had to go.

By early morning, they were once again moving through nearly deserted streets, heading for the Jaffa Gate and the road down toward the coast and the main north-south route called the Way of the Sea. From there, they would join one of the many caravans heading for the Egyptian border, finally reaching the large Jewish district of Alexandria on the Nile delta.

CHAPTER 5

Staying Behind

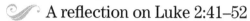 A reflection on Luke 2:41–52

*The years of growing up have their joys and pains, not
only for the young person but also for those who love him
or her and who wish to protect and guide. It is typical of
Luke's sensitivity that we get this brief glimpse linking
Jesus's childhood years in Bethlehem with the adult years
in Nazareth. Here is a moment familiar in every family,
when the emerging youth clashes with the anxiety and
protectiveness of parents . . .*

He was twelve years old. Joseph, to whom he looked as
a loving father, was still alive and active. By tradition,
Joseph was augmenting the family income by working on
the building of the new Roman center of administration in
Sepphoris, one or two hours' walk from Nazareth.

By now, Jesus had some years of schooling with the
local rabbi. For his mother, these were good years—enjoy-
able family life, dependable income, satisfaction in seeing
the children growing, the eldest helping in the workshop.
They made a big decision. It was time to take their eldest

son to Jerusalem. The neighbors even heard the grumbling resentment of Jesus's siblings!

Jesus was full of anticipation. From the moment the journey south began, he absorbed every moment of it. Along with the other young people in the caravan, they left Nazareth, coming down the hills to the Jezreel Valley, one of the loveliest parts of the country. As they turned east over to Beit Shan more travelers joined them; together they headed south along the Jordan Valley road until they reached Jericho. The winter homes of affluent Jerusalem families seemed like mansions, surrounded by orange groves.

From Jericho, the caravan crossed the floor of the valley and began the climb up the military road built by the Roman army engineers. Once atop this escarpment, Jesus had his first thrilling sight of Jerusalem.

Their journey continued through Bethany, down across the Kidron Valley, and up to one of the eastern gates of Jerusalem, where the caravan halted to deliver its goods and the travelers scattered for their various destinations and lodgings. If Jesus's grandparents—his mother's parents Anne and Joachim—were still alive in the lower city, and if their home was still available, it would provide his family with lodging for their visit. Actually, one reason for coming to the city was to check on one or both elderly grandparents. It had been some time since they had heard from them.

The city was swollen with the cosmopolitan crowds attracted by the Feast. It was intoxicating to his growing mind with endless possibilities, questions, feelings. Until now, he had known only the rural world of Galilee. He was already aware that only a few miles away from Nazareth the great caravan highways swung north of the lake, heading off for Damascus and then beyond to the infinitely remote Orient. But never had he gone down those highways, other than in imagination. Even on the journey south, the caravan had guarded them along the lonely miles where the Pax Romana could not always prevent attack or robbery.

Now in the gleaming capital, the wraps were off. The boy from Nazareth moved deeper into the labyrinth of city streets and alleys. He was mesmerized by the bustle and the crowds. All the time he was drawn by something he did not yet know.

At last he came out onto the great marble platform of Herod's temple. At least six modern city blocks long, terraced, battlemented, it was higher than a Gothic cathedral will be in the far future Middle Ages. It gleamed dazzlingly white in the Judean sun. For a Jewish boy, it was the cradle of his civilization, the sacred center of his inner universe.

As he wandered around the vast enclosure, eventually there were voices, faces, a welcome. He found rapport with the elders around him. They in turn detected something intriguing, something very unusual in this wandering boy. His youthful years of home schooling by the village rabbi had obviously given him an astonishing acquaintance with the scrolls and the great tradition of the faith. The hours went by as he discovered unrealized worlds within himself. He felt called to a journey far beyond even that of the miles he had come.

Suddenly there was an interruption. Anxious family faces appeared, their voices sharpened by fear, relief, and exhaustion. The boy felt a flicker of resentment. Imagine the eternal cry between youth and adult. Why don't they understand? Why can't they realize and accept that a voice other than theirs is calling, another relationship is demanding that he respond? To the amazement of his new temple friends, and probably to the puzzlement—even worry—of his parents, he referred to God in a most unusual way in that culture. "Did you not know," he asked, "that I must be in my Father's house?"

Before the family left the temple precincts, a wise and sensitive temple elder suggested that this unusually mature boy should be encouraged in his questions and curiosity.

As the caravan headed out of the city, a story spread: Jesus had gotten lost in Jerusalem. However, Jesus felt he simply "stayed behind in Jerusalem." He was not lost.

Was there a hint of a deliberate decision on Jesus's part to go into the warren of streets, courtyards, and shops that form the old city to this day? We might wonder further if such a decision was conscious or unconscious. Both eventualities beg a further question—why? Was something or someone, even at this early stage in Jesus's life, calling him to the great journey that would end with his calling all of us to himself?

CHAPTER 6

The Road Not Travelled

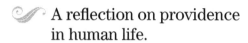 A reflection on providence
in human life.

*In our early years, there are many people who have hopes
for our lives. Those who are nearest to us and who love
us will try to point us in certain ways, subtly (or not so
subtly) encouraging us to choose a particular path. But
unknown to us, there may also be others who have their
own hopes for us. It must have been the same for Jesus
before he made the decision that changed everything . . .*

For over thirty years, Tobias had been rabbi in the village,
caring for and guiding his people. The time had come for
stepping back, but who would take over from him? He
had tried to bring the subject up with his people, but out
of affection for him they would not hear of his potential
retirement.

There came a day of particular weariness. There had
been a great deal of sickness in the village. He had been
called hither and yon to comfort and to advise. For some

reason, he found himself thinking of the great rabbi Hillel whom he remembered from the time when he himself was very young. Tobias wished the great man were still alive so that he could ask him for advice. However there was one piece of Hillel's wisdom that Tobias could easily recall, even in his exhausted state.

If I am not for myself, then who will be?
and if not now, when?
If I am for myself only, then who am I? (Pirkei Avot 1:14)

It was at that moment that he found himself thinking of one of his own congregation, the young man named Jesus, son of Mary, who had lived in the village all his life. He remembered when her husband Joseph had lost his life in an accident on a building site in the neighboring city of Sepphoris.

Memories about the family began to form. There had been some early doubt about Joseph's status as father of the child. With time, such talk had faded. Other children had followed. After Joseph's death, Jesus had stepped into the role of the eldest son to continue the business.

Tobias's thoughts turned to more recent years. The young man had always been faithful to the synagogue. He had a quiet disposition, one that showed kindness and sensitivity, a natural caring for others. Some spoke of him as having a wisdom beyond his years. Tobias remembered a Sabbath when he had asked Jesus to read from the scroll. He could not recall the passage of scripture itself, but he did recall the young man speaking for a moment or two and quoting the well-known statement of Hillel: "What is hateful to you, do not do to your fellow: this is the whole Torah" (Babylonian Talmud, tractate Shabbat 31a).

Was it possible, thought Tobias, that the successor he had been praying to find had been seated Sabbath by Sabbath in his own synagogue? Swiftly his mind moved from possibility to certainty. It all seemed so clear! Surely this was the Lord pointing him toward where he had never thought of searching.

As quickly as his aching knees would carry him, Tobias headed for the young man's home. Over the years since Joseph's death, the small house had been given a name by the village. They had come to call it the "House of the Just Man," expressing their respect and admiration for Joseph. As Tobias toiled up the slope of the dusty road, he felt more and more certain that he had received a revelation. There was not a moment to delay.

When he reached the house, he realized that Mary had company. Two of the extended family—one of them James, Jesus's brother—were with her. Tobias saw to his consternation that Mary was weeping. He asked gently why she was weeping. When she told him, he felt a great wave of disappointment.

James helped Tobias to a chair. The old rabbi listened as he was told of Jesus's decision to leave for the south, where his cousin John was attracting crowds as he spoke compellingly of a more just society. Each time he spoke,

John would call people to prepare and commit themselves to such a future by accepting the simple but profound rite of baptism in the Jordan.

As Tobias listened to James, who himself expressed deep regret at his brother's choice, the old man bowed his head and tried to control his feelings. He had permitted himself to nurture such hope, such confidence that the Lord was pointing him to this moment. Now, it had been snatched away. But then the faithfulness and the wisdom of years made it possible for Tobias to hear the words of the prophet Isaiah, as if they were being addressed to himself at this moment.

> For my thoughts are not your thoughts,
> nor are your ways my ways, says the LORD. (Isaiah 55:8)

When James finished telling Tobias what had happened, they began to speak of other things. After a while, having accepted some simple hospitality, the old rabbi rose, gave the family his blessing, and left.

Far to the south, a solitary figure stood in the Jordan, fell back into the supporting hands of John the baptizer, then rose again. Turning away from the crowds, he waded across the shallow water to the opposite bank and disappeared into the desert.

PART II

Our Lord's Ministry

CHAPTER 7

The River

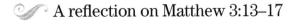 A reflection on Matthew 3:13–17

Jesus is in his late twenties. He has lived and worked in Nazareth for about fifteen years, sharing the life of the family home. But something is calling him to a larger world . . .

The voice, the sense of being addressed, became more insistent as time went by. What exactly he was being called to still eluded him. Sometimes in the evening, after the work of the day, he went into the hills to be alone, to wait for some clear signal of direction, to try to hear what something or somebody was calling him to say "yes" to. Nothing came, but of one thing he was sure. There was a Presence.

A casual remark from one of his friends in the village made all the difference. The friend had been down south for a few weeks and was very excited about a remarkable voice that was being listened to down there. The moment he heard his friend's description, he knew that this voice was actually that of his own cousin John. He had heard the rumors. It seemed that John was leading a reform movement of some kind: an extremely dangerous thing to attempt under the watchful eyes of the Roman occupation.

As his friend talked more and more excitedly, he felt pieces of the puzzle falling into place. From what he was hearing, John's preaching was harsh and strident and demanding, yet crowds were beginning to gather. John was speaking of a change coming in society, a change bigger than even the Roman occupation. Apparently even off-duty soldiers stood in the crowds, not only listening to John but asking him interested questions, obviously respecting his answers because they were clear, precise, and full of common sense. Some of John's people were concerned that he was sharing his vision too readily with these representatives of the authorities. They seemed friendly, but some in the crowd were not so sure. However, John insisted on speaking to them when they approached him.

To all this, he listened intently. He learned that his friend had joined others in responding to John's invitation. It all came pouring out as the friend relived the experience: standing in the brown swirling water, falling back in trust on waiting arms, feeling the momentary panic of the sense of drowning, then drawing breath again to stand in the bright sunlight with a sense of newness, of rising, of birth, somehow strengthened to envision and to work for the new world that John was talking about. As he listened, he could hear the enthusiasm in his friend's every word.

Suddenly he knew with absolute certainty that he must go to John. He also knew with certainty what that meant for the family. Since the death of his father Joseph, he, as the eldest, had been the family head. His mother was aging and tired. On the other hand, there were siblings old enough to keep things going. James could. He and James had always been close. James would understand.

And so a few days later, he found himself heading down toward the Jezreel, then over to Beit Shan and on down the Jordan Valley road. Each evening as he built a small fire the voices of family and friends echoed in his ears, some wishing him well but almost all warning him that this could be very unwise. Even James, who had been supportive of his wish to leave, had warned him that the country was alive with religious and political ideas and causes, some of them dangerous and radical. Still, James had encouraged him to go, saying that not to go would be to wonder for the rest of his life where life might have taken him.

The third afternoon, he found himself moving through the crowd toward the riverbank. John, standing in the water, had just finished addressing the crowd and was now offering his rite of baptism to those who wished it.

Now that he was actually here, it seemed that all his doubt and ambivalence conspired in a last-ditch effort to make him draw back. But at that very moment, he realized that John had seen him. It was years since they had met. He could sense John groping to identify him. Then came recognition, followed by a look of puzzlement and concern.

He would often recall the moment when he entered the water and waded toward John. It seemed to him that he and John were the only two people present, both of them caught in what seemed to be a world at once miniscule and yet infinite. He saw that his appearance had shaken John. Neither of them said anything until they were standing close together in the water. John still hesitated, as if unnerved by the significance of what was happening. In a hoarse anxious whisper John said, "I'm not worthy for this." Quietly but firmly he insisted that John continue. Still unwilling but resigned, John gestured and he allowed himself to fall back into the strong waiting arms.

For a moment, the brown warm water was everywhere, in his ears, his eyes, his nostrils. He was aware of a moment of panic, gasping and struggling to stand again. As he found his feet and steadied himself, feeling the water dripping from him, he was suddenly aware of what he had come to think of as the Presence. It had spoken to him repeatedly in the night hours at home and on the hillsides around the village. It had never directed, but it had called, gently yet insistently. Now it spoke with an exultant certainty.

He felt every vestige of doubt and ambivalence being swept away. In its place was an utter certainty in the rightness of his choice, in his journey south, and in his standing here beside John. He became aware that John had stepped back from him and was gazing at him with eyes that mirrored both wonder and fear, while he himself was conscious only of one thing: a peace the like of which he had never known.

He was aware of the crowd on the nearby riverbank, then of someone offering to throw him the cloak he had shed. He gestured to whomever it was and it was thrown to him. Grasping it and throwing it over his shoulder, he turned away from the crowd, said a quiet word of thanks to John, and began wading across the shallow river.

He had just stepped on to the farther bank when John, as if he could no longer control the emotional storm within him, burst out once again with a cry of unworthiness. This time the crowd heard it clearly. Turning and looking back at his cousin, he became aware of the crowd behind John, drawn by this message of hope and change, yet so fickle in their loyalty and so vulnerable to the powerful forces that ruled them. He noticed again the presence of a Roman detachment scattered here and there, keeping a low profile but still watchful. In that moment he realized, almost with pity, the immense vulnerability of John, his courage in the face of great risk.

Moved by a sudden admiration he waded back toward his cousin, placed his hands firmly on his shoulders, looked into eyes that were full of weariness, stress, and anxiety, and said quietly but very deliberately, "You are not unworthy John. You are a voice in this wilderness. You make straight the way of God for all of us." Not waiting for a response, he turned, waded again to the opposite shore, strode up the slope of the bank, and disappeared into the silence and shadows of the wadi.

CHAPTER 8

The Time of Demons

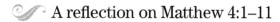 A reflection on Matthew 4:1–11

Jesus has taken what must have been a very difficult decision: to leave for the south and associate himself publicly with the reform movement of his cousin John. However, his acceptance of baptism from John has given him a sense of the inner peace he has sought for some time. He now knows himself to be called by a love beyond all human loves. He also knows that there is now no going back . . .

Today finds him in the echoing silence of the desert beyond the river. He does not yet know it, but this brutal and dangerous labyrinth of rock and sand will shape the rest of his life. The silence, the solitariness, the glittering night sky, will all conspire to reveal what lies below consciousness. The desert will bring him its demons of fear, anxiety, guilt, and self-doubt.

In the small hours, the demon comes. "If," whispers the ice-cold voice, "If you are the Son of God . . ." That chilling "if" will be repeated more than once. More than once he will ask himself if he is just imagining this call to greater things.

By now the days and nights have become weeks. The demon is still relentless. "So, you wish to change the world, do you? How? Where will you begin?" Wild possibilities come to his mind. There was a morning when the dawn sunlight made the rocks around him shine like loaves of golden bread. Why not feed the hungry and gain a following? There was a restless night when he found himself, as in a dream, on the pinnacle of Herod's temple, a vast crowd far below waiting for some gesture that would make him their political savior. Only a few nights ago, he had a delirious dream of power, power like that of Rome, even greater. The temptation was seductive.

In the last few days, he has come to realize that all the choices being offered to him are essentially the same, and that they are all equally false. All are a temptation to his ego. He alone can feed people. He alone can impress them or dominate them. In such terms the choices are presented. Now, with the awareness that all these apparent choices are delusory, he recognizes that he has the ability to dismiss the demons. Suddenly he hears himself shout out a fierce, "No!" It echoes again and again along the steep walls of the wadi.

In that instant, a very different kind of voice seems to begin to speak deep inside him, guiding him to realize that the opposites of ego, power, and domination are relationship, friendship, and community. With a surge of joy, he is aware of a new sense of purpose. A new vision has begun to form within him. The demons have faded, the desert has ceased to be a place of fear. The voice of Isaiah, learned in childhood, comes again to him. He has always loved this lyrical voice . . .

The wilderness and the dry land shall be glad,
the desert shall rejoice and blossom;
like the crocus . . . (Isaiah 35:1)

With utter clarity he knows what he will do. He will leave the desert, cross the river, and turn north up the Jordan Valley road, all doubt removed, all fear gone. He will continue north around the lake and rent a room in Capernaum. There he will rest before making his next move.

CHAPTER 9

Forming the Circle
❧ A reflection on Mark 1:16–20

*Jesus has tested the many scenarios of his desert experi-
ence. He has recognized that all of them were appeals to
the ego, to a lone high-profile future that would impress,
amaze, attract. He realizes that such a choice would be
morally bankrupt and self-defeating.*

*Now that he has returned to the familiar world of Gal-
ilee, he searches out those who will form the inner core of
what will one day become the vast People of God among
whom we ourselves find faith.*

He made his move without haste and with great care. His
first choice would be two brothers whose family have fished
the lake for generations. For a few weeks, the three of them
spent hours talking about the world they lived in and the
world they wished for. They told him about the various
choices made by some of their friends in the last couple
of years, how almost all of them had visits from the resis-
tance who call themselves Zealots. He already knows that
this choice is available to any young man in an occupied
country. He himself had been offered this choice back in his

home village. What he and these two brothers, Simon Peter and Andrew, have in common is that they have said "no" to the road of violence. He questioned them closely. Are there any others in the fishing fraternity who have made that choice to refuse violence?

They told him of two other brothers, James and John, and their father Zebedee, who was now too old for the chilly dawn world of fishing. He asked Peter and Andrew to mention him to the others. They too befriended him and they too showed interest in his dream. Andrew particularly advocated for drawing others in, doing it carefully and gradually. They told him of someone that surprised him. All of the lake boats and their catches have to be inspected for tax purposes by a local agent called Levi, someone with a reputation for honesty and decency. He too eventually said yes to the invitation to join the small circle.

The weeks went by. From time to time the two fishing families invited their friend from Nazareth to go out on the lake with them. Slowly he got the hang of the nets and the sails, winning their respect, sometimes laughing with them as he learned on the job. One evening, gathered on the shoreline around a roaring fire, supper ended, and cups still half full, he suddenly stood, raised his cup and said to them, "Follow me, my friends. Follow me and we will fish for many others."

And so it was, and so it will always be. Generation after generation he will never cease to call. The dream of the kingdom will never die. Someone will always say "yes." The community will always form.

CHAPTER 10

The Squall

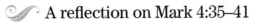 A reflection on Mark 4:35–41

In 1986, the level of the Lake of Galilee dropped sharply because of a lasting drought. Two brothers, Moshe and Yuval Lufan, whose family had fished the lake for generations, were exploring the newly revealed shoreline of the lake. There in the mud, its wooden ribs clearly visible, was a boat.

When examined by experts from Israel Antiquities, it was dated from about 50 BCE to 50 CE, thereby becoming of immense interest to both Jews and Christians: for Jews because it is a vivid and precious artifact from their history; for Christians because this is the kind of boat that would have been familiar to those fishermen whom Jesus called to be his trusted friends and disciples.

It took nearly two frantic weeks to raise the boat before the level of the lake rose again. Infinite care had to be taken not to damage the millennia-old wood. Finally, it was placed in a chemical bath for no less than ten years before being displayed in a specially acclimatized hall in the Yigal Allon Museum in Kibbutz Ginosar.

For the last three years of his life, Jesus lived in the small fishing village of Capernaum at the north end of the Lake of Galilee. The lake itself is not large, about twelve kilometers long and about four kilometers wide. For small fishing boats, especially if they are laden with a morning's catch, the north end of the lake can be dangerous. Sudden bursts of wind from the west can rush down the valley that opens on to the lake, turning its calm surface into wild and dangerous water. At that time, the shoreline of the lake was densely populated with a number of small villages whose people lived in various ways off the lake.

Very early on a lovely morning in 1990 I came to Kibbutz Ginosar. At that time the boat and its huge tank of preserving fluid were still in a plain simple shed. Only a few of us were there at that early hour. Moving around the tank and looking down into its depths, I could see the small stern area. In front of it, I could see the section of the boat designed to seat four rowers.

At this point I recall my mind conducting a silent dialogue with itself. One voice pointed out that there was absolutely no evidence that this was indeed the boat that might have belonged to James and John bar Zebedee, or to their friends Simon Peter and his brother Andrew. However, another voice responded that there was no evidence to tell me that it was not that same boat. Torn between these two voices, I found it impossible to look down through the protective liquid without recalling that it was on such a stern that Jesus, probably exhausted, and quite possibly fighting seasickness, was trying to get some sleep. In Mark's gospel

I read that he had a cushion. I could well understand why he needed it! Thoughts like this drew me back across the centuries to that long-ago day.

It was not difficult to hear a voice shouting for someone to take down the sail, then the scraping of baskets hastily grabbed to throw the valuable catch over the side to heighten the boat in the water. Obviously they survived and would certainly have talked about it. Years later John Mark would include the incident in his gospel; by then it would have gone through many tellings. I suspect that countless children were put to bed by the story of Jesus and his disciples on a stormy lake.

Meanwhile, back on the boat that day, I wonder if, because they cared for him and knew how exhausted he was, they delayed as long as possible before waking him. In the end, they simply had to wake him because they needed every hand available, and Jesus was the one who was in a position to provide the extra strength to control the steering oar on which their safety ultimately depended.

What they never forgot is how he responded. Years later, it was Peter who described the moment to John Mark. At no time did Jesus show fear, and his extraordinary calm communicated itself to the others. I can't help wondering if Peter ever joked that because Jesus was the only non-fisherman in the boat, his amazing calm in the face of very real and present danger was simply due to the fact that he didn't realize how precarious the situation actually was. If Peter ever did make that joke, I can just as easily imagine Jesus responding with a laugh. As the years go by and the telling is passed on and on, perhaps the story gets richer and richer until Jesus's bidding his friends to keep calm is transformed into his addressing and calming of the storm itself.

To surmise this is not in any way to diminish the beauty and power of this passage in Mark's gospel. The fact is that down through time, countless souls reading or listening to this passage in the gospel have been calmed, strengthened, and comforted as they themselves experience the storms of life.

CHAPTER 11

Suppliant and Healer

❧ A reflection on Matthew 15:22–29

In the film version of the play Jesus Christ Superstar *there is a desert scene in which Jesus heals those who come to him. More and more come and he tries desperately to keep up, until he is eventually overcome by sheer numbers. The last moment shows his arm outstretched under a mound of writhing humanity.*

The gospels do not try to hide those times when Jesus feels he must move away for at least a few days from the crowds that follow him with their endless needs and pleading and demands. It would seem that he liked to cross the lake to the quiet eastern shore, but on this one occasion he heads northwest into what today we call Lebanon. Here he encounters a woman of the area who pleads that this now well-known rabbi heal her daughter . . .

She was sitting in her doorway weeping, her arms around her daughter, after one of the frightening seizures that had become part of the family's life, when a neighbour came running. A healer whose name had become a byword in the province to the south had been seen in the area. No sooner did she hear the news than she knew what she had to do, even if it meant leaving the child with neighbors. As a woman, her journey alone would be dangerous, but there was no other way.

Two days later she intercepted the group. At first she kept her distance. Eventually one of them approached her. He asked her what she wanted. She told him. His voice hardened. The healer was not accepting any requests. He was exhausted and badly needed rest.

Desperation drove her. She kept pace behind them. She kept calling out her need, trying to catch the ear of the healer.

Toward evening they stopped. One of them again approached her. She steeled herself for what might come, but this time it was different. The healer would see her. She burst out crying and ran toward him, throwing herself before the seated figure. She could see immediately that he was indeed exhausted.

Eyes glazed with weariness looked at her. A voice hoarse from dealing with crowds said quietly, "You know of course that my work is over there." A hand pointed wearily to the southeast. She nodded, aware only that he was at least talking to her. She gasped out her need: the fevers, the terrible spasms, her journey south, her fear for the child, her certainty that unless he responded to her the child would surely die. She knew also that if he chose to he could make all the difference. All of this was gasped out between great sobs of exhaustion from the journey, but also from years of struggling with this demon that had invaded their lives.

There was silence. He looked away from her toward the distant sea. They could hear the booming of the Rosh Hanykra grotto, where the ocean thundered through the rocks. She kept silent, fearful that her link with him would be broken. When he did turn back to her and speak, his words at first terrified her because they seemed to speak of refusal. "It is not fair," he said quietly, "to take the children's food and cast it to the dogs."

She felt a moment of utter despair. Only when their eyes met did she see a kindness that hinted of invitation, an invitation to her to respond. For a moment she couldn't think, then she heard herself say, "But even the dogs eat of the crumbs that fall from their master's table."

The tired face broke into a smile. Afterward, when she would recall the encounter as she did countless times, she thought she may have heard him say a quiet, "Thank you." She was never quite sure of that, but she would never forget the moment when he extended his hand towards her and gave her the promise of the child's healing.

She would journey north again, this time in hope. She would see the village, see a hand waving. She would be met by friends among whom the slight figure of her daughter stood ready to receive a mother's embrace.

As time went by and the daughter grew, her mother would ask for news of the healer. There came the day when she was told of his death by some passing visitors to the village. But there was one thing she could never know. She would never know that the image she had blurted out in desperation, the image of hungry mouths scrambling for crumbs under a family table, would become the central image for what many consider the loveliest and most valued of all prayers far in the future.

She would never know that generation after generation, century after century, millions would fall on their knees, their voices echoing her voice, seeking the presence of the healer who once looked into her eyes and who would become the healer of the world. " . . . We are not worthy so much as to gather up the crumbs under thy table. But thou art the same Lord, whose property is always to have mercy. . . ."*

This she would never know, but we know. As she knelt, so we kneel. As her child was healed, so we are healed. Thanks be to God.

---

* "The Prayer of Humble Access" in *The Book of Common Prayer,* 337.

CHAPTER 12

The One Who Came Back

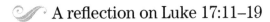 A reflection on Luke 17:11–19

For eighteen months he has been renting a room in this house in the small lakeside village called Capernaum. He is about to do what he doesn't want to do. He feels he has to go south. Jerusalem is the heart of this small world he lives in. The temple is the place where he must be seen and heard from time to time if he is to have any public recognition. He is aware that deep within himself, he doesn't like the city and all that it represents in terms of power and political sophistication, even corruption. But he also knows he must make this journey. A few friends have said they can get away to go south with him . . .

As he closed the door on the small room he had been renting, he found himself wondering if he would ever be back. That thought stayed with him as he walked to meet his companions at the appointed rendezvous. In the distance to the south, the foothills of Samaria caught the rays of the morning sun.

About noon they crossed the fertile fields of the Jezreel Valley. They had just skirted a small village when they saw the group clustered together beside the road. The dark mass of misshapen bodies and filthy clothing was familiar. As they came nearer the group they saw there were ten people, mostly men, a few women; ten human lives. He knew these ten men and women were once active and enjoying life with those whom they loved. Now everything was changed for them. Everything and everybody they had ever held dear had been lost to them because of the dreaded lesions of leprosy on their bodies. So, forbidden by law to approach anyone, the group made no move toward the passing strangers and the rabbi.

Stepping away from his companions, the rabbi went toward the group. Instantly the lepers knew that this rabbi was prepared to ignore the terrible isolation imposed on them. In that long-ago society, even to be approached by another healthy human being was a gesture of healing—at least emotional healing.

As he walked forward he knew that by law the only way these people could have any hope of recovering their lives was to be examined by a priest and pronounced clean. But this rabbi also knew that the priests could sometimes be wrong in their diagnosis. He knew that the term "leprosy" covered many kinds of skin infections, some much less serious than others. Experience had taught him to watch for such things. As he approached the group he looked for signs here and there that some might have lesser infections than others.

Then he did the unthinkable. He gently touched the signs of actual leprosy in one of them. In doing so, he challenged the heart of the legal system. The law was absolutely categorical: no healthy person was to go within one hundred and fifty yards of a leper.

There then came the moment when he told them to do what the law directed: to show themselves to a priest. He warned that some might be disappointed, but he also knew that some non-leprous lesions might have healed spontaneously or at least have begun the healing process. As well, some would have been wrongly diagnosed. To know this at least gave hope. There was some anxious questioning of the rabbi, demands for reassurance, but eventually farewells were exchanged and the group moved away in the direction of the nearest village to where they might find a priest.

Meanwhile, the rabbi and his small group of friends continued their journey south toward Jerusalem. Late in the evening they located a suitable place to spend the night. While they were sharing the evening meal, a solitary figure walked into their encampment out of the surrounding darkness. The stranger was exhausted and hungry.

Throwing himself in front of the rabbi, laughing and weeping in his joy, he blurted out his repeated thanks. If the rabbi had not given him the courage to risk an examination, he would never have dared to undertake the fateful journey. Again and again he offered his gratitude. Only then would he accept hospitality, followed by the offer of a place around the embers of the fire against the rising cold of the night hours.

Before they slept, the rabbi gestured to the overjoyed stranger to sit beside him. Speaking to them all quietly, he said, "Others were healed. I wonder where they are? Our friend here, who has come back to us, and who has poured out his thanks—isn't it very interesting that he is actually a Samaritan? How infinitely sad it is that most people consider him to be an absolute outsider."

In the small group around the fire there was silence. All realized that the one whom they called Master had just challenged their deepest humanity.

PART III

Our Lord's Passion

CHAPTER 13

The Choice

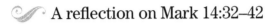 A reflection on Mark 14:32–42

*On Thursday morning in Holy Week 1993 I am scheduled
to be with a group of clergy in the Church of St. Peter in
Gallicantu (Cock Crow), south of the Old City in Jerusalem. Perhaps because of the mid-morning hour, the traffic
is light and the taxi brings me to the church with a little
time to spare. I open the door slightly to check that my
group is already there and a colleague is just finishing a
lecture on the history of the site . . .*

I closed the door quietly and walked to a point beyond the
church from where I was looking east down a long grassy
slope that drew my eyes first to the Tyropean valley, then
up the lower slopes of the Mount of Olives, and finally to
its summit.

I knew that in our Lord's day the worn ancient steps
below me, now half hidden in the soil, provided a way for
people to climb from the lower to the upper city. As my
eyes focused on the south end of the Tyropean valley, I
recalled that many think it likely that the house where our
Lord shared supper with his friends was somewhere in that

area. As I looked beyond to the Mount of Olives, I recalled that at that time it would have been thickly wooded.

At that moment I had an experience I have never forgotten, giving me a sense of the presence of Jesus as nothing else ever has. Because it was Holy Thursday, I began to imagine what that long-ago Thursday must have been like for him. I thought about how painful that evening meal must have been for him, first because of the looming shadow of a dreadful death, but also because of the knowledge that he had been betrayed by a close friend. Then I remembered that late in the meal he suggested that they leave the house and move toward the lower slopes of the Mount, to what in those days was a public garden area.

During that walk, Jesus seemed to change his mind about wanting the full band of the disciples to accompany him. He indicated that he wished for only a few to continue with him. Then, taking with him Peter, James, and John, he proceeded further up the slope. He paused once again, turned to the three, and asked them to allow him to go on alone.

Whether he continued into the wooded area only a short distance—Mark speaks of Jesus going "a little farther"—or whether they kept him in sight because of their concern for his obvious distress, we will never know, but we do have a record of the agonized struggle that took place in that dark rock-strewn clearing. We also know the sublime climax of that struggle, as Jesus says to the Father, ". . . not what I want, but what you want."

As I stood at the railing that morning, I recalled that I had a small testament in my shoulder bag. I took it out and found the relevant passage in the gospel. As I did so I became aware of a pattern. I became almost certain that the sequence in our Lord's behavior—needing the company of friends, then wishing for only a few, then wanting to be alone, then returning three times only to find them asleep—portrayed him struggling with a decision that he dare not share with any of them, even those closest to him.

I looked again at the Mount of Olives, trying to imagine it as it was that night. The upper slopes would have led deeper and deeper into trees and thick undergrowth. Had he chosen, an active thirty-year-old could have reached that summit very quickly. From there he could be far out in the Judean desert in an hour or two.

It is highly unlikely he would have been pursued. If Jesus had indeed fled, a seasoned politician like Caiaphas would have known that there was no need whatsoever to bother with pursuit. By fleeing, the teacher from Galilee would have forfeited any possibility of ever again leading a significant political or religious movement. The chief priest would actually have been relieved that it was no longer necessary to disturb the Passover season and embarrass the procurator by insisting on a high-profile trial.

I cannot help but think Jesus had to wrestle with this temptation. If I am to accept his utter humanity, then I have to assume that he dreaded the hideous death that he knew was imminent. But as I stood by the railing on that Holy Thursday I also knew that I stood there as a Christian only because he did not give into the temptation to flee. For this, you and I and millions of Christians are inexpressibly grateful.

CHAPTER 14

Standing By

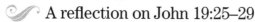 A reflection on John 19:25–29

Now there stood by the cross of Jesus his mother, and his mother's sister, Mary the wife of Clopas, and Mary Magdalene . . .

When the young Roman guard asked them to keep back from the area, she noticed that he was little more than a boy. The thought occurred to her that he must feel vulnerable at such moments as this. Around them milled a crowd, among them friends and family of the condemned, some half crazed with grief. If the prisoner was political there was the possibility of a rescue attempt, especially in the early stages of the crucifixion process.

She had arrived in Bethany too late to meet her son before he had left for the city with his followers. She felt a passing twinge of resentment, but she put it aside. By then she was used to coming second to the demands of what he regarded as his ministry. As she tried to get some rest, she heard the visitors coming and going in the house, but she knew she was being allowed to rest because there was no good news to tell her.

Very late at night, they woke her to let her know that he had been taken. As the young man told her of the impending trial, she knew that he was deliberately refraining from telling her of the possibility of execution. To her own surprise, she found herself comforting him. When he asked her what she wished to do when the time came, she said calmly that she wished to go to wherever her son would be. Again, she tried to get some sleep.

In the early morning she left with her sister and the young woman from Magdala whom she barely knew. As she walked the last few hundred yards toward the area where the crosses stood in the ground, they seemed to grow in height. When she was close enough to see features she forced herself to look. She was glad of an arm supporting her.

At first a wild hope grasped her that it was not her son at all. The body was revealed in total degradation and defilement. She found herself thinking that it was no worse than countless others had suffered. Like most people she had always avoided any acquaintance with the obscene process of crucifixion.

As the young Roman guard ordered them to keep their distance, they shuffled back some yards. She looked across the filthy ground between them and the crosses. It occurred to her that all her life she had been distanced from her son. Even when she and Joseph brought him as a child to the temple, she had to look across a barrier as the priest took the baby and later returned him. Almost always it was across barriers, walls, chasms, and crowds that their relationship had been conducted and their elusive love communicated. Of one thing she was certain: that he had loved her. Even if they had not often spoken it, she knew it to be real and lasting.

Someone told them it had been a long time since the execution had begun. It now looked as if the end was not far off. By now the front of the crowd had inched forward again. She was aware with mingled terror and joy that he had opened his eyes and seemed to have seen them. She could see his lips moving, trying to form some word. Careless now of any restraint she moved forward to try to catch the sound.

When the faint croaking sank to silence she moved back. In that moment, by the whispered statement of her dying son, this young man who had joined them and now stood beside her, had somehow become her son, and she his mother. This evidence of her own son's concern for her, even in his extreme agony, was for her a mingling of pain and appreciation.

With the help of her sister and the young woman from Magdala who had come with them, she began to move away. She never heard the terrible cry of desolation that took all but his last breath.

As she departed, she recalled the old man Simeon tenderly returning her newborn son to her arms in the temple all those years ago. She remembered him looking at her intently as he spoke very quietly. "One day," he had said, "a sword will piece your heart."

One day. . . . To a new young mother it had sounded so far in the future, and anyway she had no idea what the old man meant. Even now, as she left the hillside, she was not aware that in an hour, a Roman lance would pierce her son's side.

As they continued down the hill she almost fell on the treacherous path, had not her sister and the young woman of Magdala supported her.

CHAPTER 15

Stranger on the Road

A reflection on Luke 24:13–35

*It is the first day of the week in a bustling Jerusalem, but
for a small community that has experienced the tragic loss
of their leader it is a day of intense sorrow shot through
with an agonizingly elusive hope. Two of the community,
returning home in despair, have an encounter that changes
everything . . .*

Looking at him across the room, she could see her husband Cleopas was exhausted. She knew she was certainly approaching her own emotional limits. The two of them had come in from Emmaus a week ago, knowing that the family would need support as things got steadily worse for her sister Mary and her son. Over the last seventy-two hours, the horror on the hill where she had witnessed indescribable agony, would, she knew, send her over the edge if she didn't do something to keep control.

They had decided to stay with the group in Jerusalem to be near family, but she knew this could not continue. Everyone around her was on edge. It was simply not wise to stay.

Apart from anything else, they needed to go home to look after things. It was now a week since they had come to the city. So much had happened, so many awful things, that it seemed much longer, but it was time to go home. Emmaus was only a long walk away, over the hills. She was grateful Cleopas and herself could still do it.

They had left the city behind and were about halfway home when they became aware that someone was walking behind them on the road. Cleopas was about to turn around when they were addressed from the gathering dusk.

"Well, you two are obviously deep into some discussion. May I ask what it's about or would I be trespassing?" The voice was pleasant, easy, almost jocular. Perhaps it was the quality of ease that seemed to trigger a nerve in her husband. The tone was in such absolute contrast to their own grief. Cleopas's response was petulant and resentful, so much so that she half expected the stranger to be repelled. However, he persisted in a tone that encouraged even Cleopas to relent and enter into a conversation as they continued along side by side.

Over the next couple of miles, their despair and agony poured out: the recent years spent with a wonderful person, the dreams and hopes, the final horror, the tantalizing and mysterious hints of the last few hours. All through it they walked together, the stranger listening intently, saying nothing.

Then came his response. When it did, it was so sustained, reassuring, and revealing that only long afterward would they realize that he had given them a completely new lens through which to understand the great tradition they had been brought up in as children. As they listened, even the pain and loss started to make sense. Somehow, a mysterious healing seemed to begin.

She could see that Cleopas felt as she herself did. Neither of them wanted this encounter to end. Both began to blurt out the invitation at the same moment. Would he share a meal? Of course. An inn? Of course. Being from the area they knew one nearby. She would have preferred to suggest their own home but there was nothing to offer a guest after their having been away for so long.

Every moment of what followed would become indelible memory. The table in the cool darkness of the inn, the wooden platter of fresh homemade bread put down by the landlord's daughter, the relaxed, almost languid movement of the stranger's hands lifting a piece of bread, the quiet almost inaudible blessing, the breaking, the offering, their own instinctive reaching toward him, all would remain etched for ever in memory.

Nothing further was said. She felt captive—a willing, joyful captive—to this moment. She could see and feel that the same was true for Cleopas. The silence continued for what seemed an eternity of deepening wonder and inexpressible joy.

Held in the silence, they were dimly aware that the stranger was gently excusing himself and withdrawing from them. Neither she nor Cleopas moved. It seemed somehow right for them to remain still within the mystery of the moment. The open doorway darkened for a moment in what she later thought of as his leaving. Then he was gone. Neither of them moved. When they dared to look at one another, their eyes were brimming with tears.

Hours later, having turned back toward the city, they would find themselves among the others, desperately trying to control themselves sufficiently to relate coherently what had taken place.

CHAPTER 16

Fire on the Lakeshore

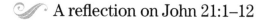 A reflection on John 21:1–12

Weeks have passed since the weekend that had changed everything. Their hopes have been shattered, their friend and leader killed in the cruelest possible way. They have also shared experiences that were beyond understanding yet were, they felt, utterly real. By now, those who had gone south to be with him in those last days have left Jerusalem and returned home to their villages in Galilee. They are traumatized by all that they have experienced and are finding it difficult to resume the familiar pattern of their working lives . . .

It was Peter who suggested that they might once again take up the threads of normal life. Weeks had passed since the terrible death on the hill. Something unforgettable had ended; nobody knew what was beginning. Sometimes they even doubted their own experiences in Jerusalem, far to the south of these Galilean hills and the blue lake and the villages. It sometimes seemed that it could all have been a nightmare of mingled terror and wonder. As the days passed it began, as all dreams do, to fade. It did not help to have to respond to well-meaning neighbors and extended family who sometimes communicated sympathy at the naivete of following the inflated dreams of yet another self-proclaimed messiah. One morning, they agreed to go out on the lake. Long afterward John, by then an old man, recalled the moment that changed their lives.

They were near the shore. Normally the beach would have been clearly visible, but on this particular day there was a thick morning mist. One of them noticed what might have been a fire lit on the shingle. Curious because it was so early, they kept glancing at the flames. It was John whose intuition pierced the fog in a way that sight could not.

At that moment a voice came across the shrouded, glassy water. "Children, you have no fish, have you?"

Instinctively responding to the authority of the voice they gave a ragged shout, "No!" A reply came immediately. "Cast the net to the right side of the boat." They did so without question as if under some kind of spell. The water began to heave and splash around them, releasing them into frenzied activity.

It was John's voice that rang out, high and clear. "It is the Lord!" For a moment they were held by fear, joy, disbelief, awe. A strangled sound came from Peter's throat, then he was over the side, up to his armpits in the water, grabbing the bow rope and wading frantically for the shore.

So, in the dawn light, they met their Lord, but there was a strange contradiction about the moment. John recalled that he was quite certain he was in the presence of Jesus whom he had followed as teacher and friend, yet in a way quite beyond description he also knew that it was no longer the same quality of presence. As they shared a meal on the beach together, John realized something more was among them, something wondrous.

After they had shared the meal, Jesus gestured to Peter to walk apart with him. The rest stayed around the fire.

As they walked down the beach, no word was spoken. Peter himself was conscious of only one thing: the last occasion on which he and Jesus had been together. He had looked across a courtyard in the chief priest's house as Jesus emerged from brutal questioning. Peter had chosen to stay in the area in spite of the danger, but had to deny any knowledge of the prisoner if he was to avoid involvement.

All through the terrible days of trial and execution, Peter had been compelled to live with that guilt. Now, still not knowing if this was a dream from which he would awaken, he became aware that Jesus was speaking to him about their relationship, speaking insistently and urgently. No word was mentioned about any past betrayal. Three times Peter was asked for his complete loyalty, and three times he gave it fervently. To the third asking he responded passionately. Each time he did so, Jesus looked toward the group along the beach and commended them to Peter's leadership and care. Peter was utterly overcome by the affirmation he was receiving.

There was a strange moment when they saw John walking down the beach toward them. Peter had never felt comfortable in the presence of this younger man who was so different from him. Suddenly he found himself voicing these misgivings to Jesus, only to have his fears dismissed and to be met once again with affirmation and assurance. John had his gifts and they would be used in the great work; meanwhile Peter's gifts were just as essential for the building of the community.

Here in the dawn light by the lake, Peter realized he had been given back his integrity, his confidence, his self-esteem. He had been forgiven.

In the months and years after this lakeside encounter, they would struggle for language to communicate the experience. Over the next six weeks or so there would be other encounters. Then gently but firmly, under the great arch of the sky, these encounters would come to an end.

PART IV

Letters
Lost and Newly Found

CHAPTER 17

The Expectant Mother

A reflection on Luke 1:39–56

In the early days of her pregnancy, our Lord's mother may well have had to endure gossip and innuendo in the small world of her village. At some point in those early days, she made a decision. She had become aware that an older cousin who lived in the hill country of north Judea was also unexpectedly pregnant. Mary decided to get away to where she could rely on understanding and affection, rather than snide questioning and criticism.

The journey south would not have been easy and could have been even dangerous. We can presume she joined a caravan for safety. She realized too she would face the return journey as her pregnancy advanced. I found myself wishing to explore that time after her return, assuming that the visit had been a success . . .

My dearest cousin Elizabeth,

I apologize for not sending this letter earlier. I was exhausted from the journey home and simply had to rest for the last few days. I think about you and pray for you constantly, because I know you were very near to giving birth when I had to leave. As you know, I had no choice when the caravan came through the village and they told us there wouldn't be another for nearly a month. However, I could see that you had friends ready to help, so I'm assuming my prayers for you have been answered.

My journey, thank God, was safe and uneventful. I have always been led to believe that Samaria could be unfriendly and even dangerous. Instead, I found much friendship from the villages we passed through.

The most fascinating part of my journey home was to see Sepphoris. Our caravan left me there because it was going on around the lake and not through Nazareth. You and Zechariah have never seen it, but you can imagine what it's like when I tell you it's the new headquarters for the Roman administration of Galilee. Beautiful streets and houses, lovely mosaics, chariots coming and going everywhere.

But you'll never guess the really wonderful thing that happened. Joseph was there to meet me! I was hoping he could, but we were not sure it was possible. As I told you, Sepphoris is only two hours walk from Nazareth and the army contract that he's been working on has been extended.

To have a few days together was wonderful. Sepphoris is big enough that hardly anybody knew us. Well, a few did, because like my Joseph, they had come over from Nazareth to find jobs. The really nice thing about meeting them— and it made all the difference for me—was that because they were friends of Joseph, and because they had heard from him that we were going to marry, they could not have been friendlier. That meant so much to me because I had been nervous about going back to the village.

Elizabeth, I will never be able to thank you for those wonderful weeks you gave me, especially in the first few days after I arrived sick and miserable from the journey. What helped was that you were overjoyed about your own pregnancy. I could see it in your face and hear it in your voice when you came to the door to meet me. I will never forget the hug you gave me.

By now you may have given birth. Do please write soon. Send the letter with the next caravan. I've given you the name of the street and the construction site in Sepphoris—so that Joseph will get it and bring it to me. Remember, I want to know everything. All I know at the moment is that Zechariah wants it to be a boy and wants him to be called John.

Don't forget to tell me how Zechariah is. When I left he seemed to be improving from that incident in the temple that robbed him of his speech. My hope and prayer is that he may be so overjoyed when you give birth that it will give him back his voice.

Since coming home, I have learned how wonderful it is to have friends. Joseph's family have rallied around us, and even though I am sure that there are those in the village who are prepared to be hurtful—as you yourself warned me would be the case—I feel surrounded by love.

The only thing that I'm worried about is a rumor that Joseph tells me is going around in Sepphoris. He's heard from one of the army contractors that the authorities in

Rome may be planning an imperial census. If that's true, then Joseph will have to go back to his own area—down south near Bethlehem. He has said that he will not go without me because of the coming birth. I hope against hope that this doesn't happen before I give birth. The journey will be ghastly.

Elizabeth, I must end, but not without reminding you about when we spoke of our angels. Sometimes when I find it hard to sleep, my angel comes. Not that I see anything, of course. It's just that in the darkness I'm aware of a presence. I don't mean the babe, although he is very much a presence inside me. But this other presence is always reassuring and somehow familiar, as if we had met before. Sometimes I think I hear a quiet voice saying what he said the first time, "Do not be afraid, Mary." When I hear that, sleep comes.

My love to you and to Zachariah and to the babe. Maybe our sons will meet one day; perhaps they will do great things together. Let it be as God wills.

Mary

CHAPTER 18

The Customs Officer

A reflection on Matthew 2:13–23

A church Christmas card for 2017 on my desk shows a line of refugees moving across a barren landscape. One of the archetypal images of recent years has been of men, women and children moving across borders—even across oceans—in a desperate search for a livable life, even for life itself.

It's easy to forget that the decent, faithful man we know as Joseph had to make the searing decision to trust his family to a dangerous journey, if their newborn son was to survive the death squads of Herod. Joseph had only to look east from Bethlehem to the Herodium, the great looming fortress of Herod, only four miles away. They had no choice. They had to become refugees.

So, let us imagine that somewhere on the northern Sinai border with Gaza there was an Egyptian customs post on the north/south caravan road known as the Way of the Sea. Suppose the local customs officer has just had a letter from headquarters in Alexandria, requesting

information about a couple with a child who had come
through some weeks before. Suppose this customs officer,
like many minor officials in a distant posting, feels that
head office has no idea of the realities out on the edge
of empire. We can imagine him sitting down to write a
letter . . .

Sinuhe, customs officer in northern Sinai, to His Excellency Amen Ho Tep, chief commissioner of immigration

Greetings, Your Excellency.

There was a long delay in your letter reaching us here at the northern border. Your courier—who unfortunately was sent without an escort—was killed by the bandits that continually attack travelers on the coast highway between here and the Nile delta. The letter only reached us because it was taken from his body by one of our people who has infiltrated the group.

Many refugees move through this post. Most are on their way to Alexandria where, as you know, there is a large Jewish community. Most are fleeing a vicious regime that survives only because of some grim realities.

There is a large underclass that is becoming more and more impoverished, and a rich mercantile and landowning class that supports the regime of Herod, partly because it is in their best interests to do so and partly because they fear him. He survives thanks to the presence of an occupying Roman force, the elite levels of which detest him, but regard him as useful for his ruthlessness in keeping the peace. A well-paid security organization has infiltrated the population and stifles any signs of dissent.

A series of megaprojects, strategically positioned from north to south of the country, mainly defense installations, provides jobs in a purely artificial way. Because Herod is aging and ill, he is paranoid about the possibility of a rival claimant for power. He has already killed more than once, even in his own family circle.

Your Excellency, the family you write about were interviewed some weeks ago, as are all who arrive here at the border. They had fled their village just in time to escape a massacre of children. The father would not say how he had been warned. They had come south over the hills to avoid possible pursuit, and they had skirted carefully along the edge of the desert. Eventually they would have had to come out to the highway to approach this customs post.

It was obvious they had brought almost nothing with them. The woman was in her late teens or early twenties, the man about ten years older. Their child was just a few weeks old. They were exhausted from the journey, particularly the young mother. The child looked weak and undernourished.

They had no documents and almost no resources. They were fortunate that your new immigration policies had not yet reached us here to be implemented. Those changes, had we known about them, would have meant this family would have been denied entry. In this case, however, they were allowed to proceed.

They said they were heading for Alexandria, where they have extended family and so would have help settling. The man hoped to get a job with his carpentry skills. They said that like many in their situation, they would check out conditions at home from time to time by talking to later arrivals or risking the odd careful letter. When questioned about their length of stay in Egypt, they said that if conditions in their own country improved, or the regime changed, they would probably try to return home to their northern village of Nazareth.

Meanwhile, it will be of interest to your office that a small group of Herod's militia arrived here at the post about a week ago, enquiring about a family. The description they gave fit this refugee family we had admitted. When I told them that the family had gone through the border some weeks before, they saw no point in pursuit. They turned and rode back to give their report.

My personal impression of the family when I interviewed them was of decent honest people who will, I think, make good citizens—that is if they survive the dangers of the coastal journey to the Nile and decide to settle in Egypt.

With respect, Your Excellency,

I am Sinuhe your servant, senior agent in Sinai.

CHAPTER 19

The Revenue Agent

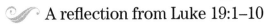 A reflection from Luke 19:1–10

*One day at the height of his short-lived popularity, Jesus
passed through the city of Jericho, probably on his way
to Jerusalem. In the large crowd that gathered to see this
now very public figure, there was an unlikely spectator
balanced precariously on a stout tree branch that guaran-
teed him a view of the popular rabbi.*

*The spectator was in fact one of the most powerful
people in the city. Zacchaeus had been able to purchase
from the Roman administration the right to levy taxes in
the greater Jericho area. He would have been cordially
detested in his community and probably needed security
at all times.*

*As he waited that day for the rabbi, he probably
tried in vain to understand the uncontrollable urge that
brought him there against all common sense. As he did
so, something took place that would not only astonish the
community he exploited and dominated, but would some
years later come to the notice of a young Greek doctor*

who was writing the story of the new Christian movement. The doctor's name was Lucas. We know him as Luke, the gospel writer.

I have taken the liberty to imagine possible consequences in Zacchaeus's life. Here is a letter he might have written to a former colleague by the name of John bar Simeon . . .

Grace and Peace to you, John.

You will probably be astonished to hear from me after all this time. However, I write to apologize for a wrong I did to you. You will recall that you refused to carry out my wishes in the matter of some tax policies that you knew—as did I—were fraudulent. For that display of integrity, I basically destroyed you professionally.

I write now in an effort to undo that great wrong, though I know well that in these cynical times you will find it hard to believe I am being sincere. The fact is that I have become very different from the man who was your employer for some ten years or so.

John, I have been changed by an encounter that took place a few weeks ago—an encounter that I did not intentionally seek, other than placing myself in a position where I could see the person who caused all this. However, let me tell you the whole story as it happened.

Doubtless you have heard in recent months of the increasing influence of a rabbi from the Nazareth area. Normally, as you can imagine, I would have taken scant notice, but one day one of my staff mentioned that this Jesus was about to pass through town, and he would like to see him, asking to have an hour off to do this. I gave permission, turned back to what I was doing and dismissed the matter from my mind.

But for some reason, I found I couldn't concentrate. I could hear the rising murmur from the streets. Suddenly in a most peculiar way I realized I had to see this fellow. I left the office, called to one of my guards—a sad necessity for us tax agents as you know—and went into the streets.

At first, I could see nothing. As you well know, my short stature has been a trial to me all my life. I threw dignity to the winds and swung myself up on the lower branches of a nearby tree. I was just in time to see him pass. Actually, I found myself so near to him that for a moment our eyes met. Whether what happened next was sheer intuition on his part, I will never know. All I know is that I thank God for it. Quite simply he suggested I might offer him hospitality. I must have shouted out a time and pointed frantically in the direction of my house. For some reason I found myself laughing with a joy I had almost forgotten.

We met for dinner. Instinct told me it should just be the two of us. I wanted it that way, and Miriam—you remember Miriam, my wife—quite understood. We talked for a long while about many things. I found him very well informed. Looking back, I realize now that he let me do most of the talking, almost as if he were waiting for something.

There came a moment of silence. I became aware of my fingers stroking a fine goblet. Suddenly tears came. I was astonished and embarrassed. I fought them, apologizing profusely, but they simply would not stop. He said nothing. He merely waited for me to recover my composure. I heard myself trying to talk to him, blurting out all the hurts and the loneliness, the growing meaninglessness of the last few years. I realized how I had come to hate so much about myself, how costly my life had become, how many ghosts haunted me.

He listened to it all. Then he said very quietly, "I know. Now that you know, what can be done?"

I found myself offering anything but the present situation. I made promises. I would make amends. I would repay. I would apologize. On and on I went, weeping, talking, promising, weeping again.

He waited through it all. He said nothing. When I had at last subsided he suggested we take a walk outside. I knew he wished to leave and, curiously enough, I felt able to allow him to leave. Somehow, I knew we had accomplished what had been necessary. We walked for a while in silence. Then, very gently, he said, "You know what you have done, don't you?"

"I think so," I replied.

"You've discovered who you really are," he said. "You've come home." He placed his hands on my shoulders for a moment, then turned and left. I have not seen him since.

And so, I write to you John, as I have written to a few other former colleagues like yourself. There is so much I regret, so much to apologize for. I do so to you now, as to one whom I once called friend. I also include this gift.

It cannot compensate for the hurt and betrayal you experienced at my hands, but it will at least compensate for much that you lost through my deceit. At some level beyond my understanding, I know that I have been forgiven. I ask now that I might receive your forgiveness.

Your friend and colleague once, and, with God's grace, I hope again,

Zacchaeus

CHAPTER 20

The Loving Son

A reflection on John 13:21–30
and Matthew 27:3–5

*A letter arrives at the home of a student who is travel-
ing. His parents, who love him, are proud as they read
the report he sends of his activities. He is spreading his
wings, meeting interesting people, especially one fascinating figure who appeals to their son's idealism and
ambition. Perhaps they are slightly concerned that he is
becoming involved in what sounds like a political movement, but on the whole they are pleased and proud . . .*

To my parents,

Grace and peace to you from your wandering but always
loving son.

I have much to share with you since I last wrote. You
remember my telling you that I had decided to get some idea
of our country as a whole. After all, I have lived all my life
with you, Alexander and Miriam down south in Kerioth.

What astonished me was the variety of our country,
the many different attitudes about many things. I became
aware of how people felt about the Roman occupation,

some resenting it, others grateful for the order it has brought, some (mostly merchants) having done well because of it. Having said this, it is interesting how many teachers and intellectuals one meets who feel that while occupation is to be regretted, it does put all of us in touch with a larger world.

The most exciting thing that has happened for me right now is an encounter I have had in Galilee. No, Mother, not the beautiful and loving woman you want me to bring home to you as my wife someday. That will come, but not yet. Meanwhile, I have met a brilliant and charismatic rabbi. I hope you both will meet him some day. It's just possible his reputation may have already reached you in Kerioth. His name is Jesus—Jesus of Nazareth.

It's been over a year now since we met. Since then, I have become involved with the growing number of men and women who are responding to his vision and the way he articulates it. His ability to draw crowds around him makes me certain he is going to become very significant in our country's life. I hesitate to say more because I know it will worry you, but I can't help admitting that I and many others are beginning to suspect that he may be nothing less than the messiah we have all been seeking for so long. No, he is not preaching violence of any kind. Quite the opposite; his message is based on the heart of the law in which you have brought us up from childhood. Love of God and love of neighbor, that is Jesus's constant theme.

I say this because I know you will think of the many previous claims to be messiah, and the fate of those who made them. Let me assure you that Jesus is in every way very different from all the others. Anybody less like a revolutionary firebrand you could not imagine. I have been with him now long enough to observe his ability to excite and attract all kinds of people, from the humblest and poorest to even some of the leadership class. To all of them he communicates a thrilling vision of hope and reform that could transform our society.

Sometimes I worry about his attitude to his own influence. He shows no sign of forming a new party for political action. Those nearest him come from the fishing community around the lake in the central Galilee where he grew up. I am the only one of the circle from outside that area. He seems to want me as a window on a wider world. As you know, we Kerioth people, being nearer Jerusalem, tend to be aware of what's going on. That's one thing for which I will always be grateful to you, Father.

Lately I have been trying to get Jesus to see the need for a plan. I know he trusts me; not long ago he asked me if I would look after the group's funds. He is certainly not politically naïve. For instance, he has no illusions about the corruption that goes on in the temple system. While he admires some aspects of the Pharisee lifestyle, he never hesitates to point out its faults, especially the way its legalistic attitudes sometimes lessen its humanity.

Here is the big news I have to share: I have been approached by a prominent Jerusalem political figure whom, for obvious reasons, I cannot name. He and others have been observing Jesus's developing influence around the country. He has also some contacts with a senior member of the procurator's staff.

It seems that the Romans have been considering the possibility of bringing about a regime change. Rome is growing tired of dealing with the new Herodian generation, the now corrupt puppet regime they themselves installed some decades ago. They are also determined to break the power of the priesthood and the temple system. My contact in the procurator's office speaks of a growing interest in Jesus as the possible leader around whom the country might come together. They recognize his total integrity and they feel they could work with him on reforms that would bring some resolution to the never-ending tensions of the province.

Everything, of course, depends on the ability of the present procurator to steer this plan.

I have said more than once to Jesus that I see no possibility of his vision of a transformed society becoming a reality unless he is prepared to risk a political role. Try to imagine what is possible if I can persuade him. If what I dare to hope for becomes a reality, we could all find ourselves in a transformed Israel, at peace with itself, integrated peacefully into the empire, led and inspired by a person of absolute integrity, rich wisdom and deep compassion. Think of how wonderful that would be!

Father and Mother, not a word of these things must go beyond our home. To all of you there I send my fondest love.

Your ever-grateful son,

Judas

CHAPTER 21

Hidden Loyalties

A reflection on John 3:1–21
and John 19:38–42

Nicodemus appears in the gospel record when he becomes aware of the presence of a certain rabbi from Galilee who happens to be in Jerusalem. For some reason that even he himself could not understand, Nicodemus was intrigued enough to arrange a meeting. As a member of the powerful Sanhedrin, the exclusive group of men who governed the affairs of the temple and the country, Nicodemus took a most unusual step when he decided to seek out the company of a mere country rabbi and to discuss intimate matters of faith and of the spirit.

That intimate conversation left Nicodemus intrigued by Jesus's ongoing ministry, even to the point where he intervened during a meeting of the Sanhedrin. Concern was being expressed by the high priest, Caiaphas, that the Galilean's movement was beginning to threaten peace and public order. Nicodemus took issue with the high priest on a matter of legal principle.

*Much had happened since that incident. The decision
to bring the new movement to an end had been taken, its
leader had been charged, tried, and found guilty. By the
authority of the occupying Roman administration, Jesus
was condemned to be crucified.*

*We meet Nicodemus on the day of the execution. He
is in his office in the temple area. A letter from one of
his Sanhedrin colleagues, Joseph of Arimathea, lies on
his desk. Nicodemus is not entirely surprised that it has
been sent. Though they have never discussed their respec-
tive links to the Galilean rabbi and his movement, each
knows that such an association would be dangerous in the
extreme. Nicodemus has come to know that Joseph also is
not unsympathetic to the teacher.*

*He has read the letter more than once. What it speaks
of is familiar to him. What it asks of him calls for a very
careful and calculated response. However, it is one which,
unknown to Joseph, Nicodemus has actually already
made. Once again, he picks up the letter with his colleague's familiar writing . . .*

To Nicodemus, fellow councilor and friend,

I write in haste and in deepest confidence. I know that
as councilors, both of us have been informed that the Galilean rabbi is to be executed in the morning. I am deeply
distressed about this decision, as I know you must be. You
have made it plain on more than one occasion that you

regard him as a deeply spiritual human being. In this I most genuinely concur. My great regret is that I did not express this publicly as you so courageously did, even though you fully realized you risked the displeasure of Caiaphas as high priest.

One of my servants has a friend among the Galilean's followers. He informed me some months ago of your visit with Jesus when he was in the city. My servant said that your meeting gave much encouragement to Jesus and his followers at that time. The fact that his teaching had attracted a person in your position gave him and others great hope that their movement might eventually extend to those whose support would be significant enough for it to be protected, even to prosper. Alas, that was not to be.

Now to the reason for this letter written in haste. As you know from having been our guest on various occasions, my villa here in Arimathea is surrounded by a generous acreage. Recently I arranged for a private family tomb to be built on its lower slope. I am prepared to receive the Galilean's body for its first stage of burial. To give him a peaceful and dignified resting place would please and comfort me deeply.

As you can imagine, taking a body down from a Roman cross is a task fraught with danger. It is essential we do no further harm to his already lacerated and torn body. My servants have been instructed to take the utmost care as they carry out my wishes.

Now for my request to you. If you feel you cannot accede to what I ask, I shall most certainly understand. You have already demonstrated your readiness to show your support, not without risk to your position. Our friend will have died by mid-afternoon. Before then I shall be on the hill with my servants. Permission has been granted. I obtained it from the procurator's chief of staff, so there will be no interference.

Nicodemus, my request is that you might accompany me on the hill. I will be quite honest in my reasons. Given your standing both in the Sanhedrin and with the Roman administration, your presence will afford me some support, even a degree of protection, if our action is later questioned and we become politically vulnerable.

One of my servants brought this letter to your office. He has instructions to wait for your reply and to deliver it to me.

My friend, I am doing what everything in my heart and soul compels me to do. I ask for the assurance that you will stand with me on the hill. Whether or not you do so, I myself will be there. I cannot do less for him. I await your reply in hope.

Your friend, colleague, and fellow seeker,
Joseph

Placing the letter once more on the table, he steps out onto the balcony of his offices where he can look west, first to the city wall, then beyond it to the area where he knows the execution is proceeding. He then turns and looks at the large jar that stands within his reach on the table. Even before receiving Joseph's letter he had pur-

chased the finest embalming materials money could buy, meaning to take it to the hill and give it to those who he knew would take the Galilean's body into their care.

His mind goes back to the evening of the encounter. There was a moment in their conversation that he vividly recalls. The Galilean had looked at him, then in a gentle chiding way, had said "Nicodemus, you may be a ruler in Israel but there are many things of the spirit you yet don't know."

How utterly true, he thinks. But there is one thing he now knows. He knows that whatever the consequences, he must now prepare to go to the hill. Once again he steps onto the balcony, this time looking down to the courtyard below, where he can see Joseph's waiting courier. At Nicodemus's call the man stands and looks up.

The message is short, clear and decisive. "Tell your Master I shall be with him on the hill."

CHAPTER 22

The Greek Tutor

A reflection on Acts 2:1–13

It is still only some weeks since the small core of Jesus's followers experienced the trauma of his terrible death. During these weeks there have been instances of individuals and groups becoming aware of his presence with and among them. So real have these experiences been that the community is now speaking of Jesus as risen.

On the occasion of the Jewish harvest festival, the community gathers in what may be the same large upper room where Jesus had celebrated Passover with his disciples such a short time previously. What takes place is remembered by Christians across the world as the birth date of the Christian church, a day celebrated in wind and fire . . .

Greetings Andronicus,

I write to share some interesting news from Jerusalem. You recall my telling you that I secured a post with an affluent Jewish family who had decided they wished a Greek tutor for their son John Mark. The boy—really almost a young man—is an excellent student.

The parents are very fine: gracious, cultured, pious. The father is a successful merchant and has travelled extensively. The mistress of the house is a charming woman. I stay in a wing of their villa.

My real news is that the life of this house has been turned upside down by events here in Jerusalem. As you know, this country is always alive with religious ideas and movements. This time it is about a movement that began in the north of the country. On the surface its leader and his ideas seemed harmless, yet his call for changes in both personal and political life are now disturbing what is always a potentially volatile society. All this continues in spite of his recent tragic death.

The concern in this house is that its mistress has become linked with the movement. We have even had some gatherings of devotees of the rabbi Jesus here, gatherings that have not gone unnoticed by people in the area. The rabbi himself, by the way, was from the much more liberal north of the country. I suspect he was not a particularly sophisticated political animal in a very political jungle. Be that as it may, the fact is that this family is now deeply in crisis.

It seems the rabbi had come south to probe the support for his movement in Jerusalem. I hear his friends watched helplessly as he clashed viciously with the authorities in public debate. The dreadful week climaxed with his trial and execution.

Before that tragic ending, however, the risk to this family increased. The mistress of the house, against the expressed wishes of her husband, actually invited the rabbi to have a meal in their home with the inner circle of his movement. Hours later he was taken, swiftly tried, and then executed.

Since then, the house has been a center for his followers. Other families have been careful to keep as low a profile as possible, in case they are seen to be involved with the new movement. There is a rumor that even among the country's governing council there are those who are sympathizers.

The extraordinary thing that has happened over the last six weeks is the growing conviction among some members of the community that the rabbi is alive, both in their personal and even in their shared experience.

Opinions about this possibility naturally differ widely. Some react patronizingly. "After all," they say, "given what these people have been through, it's understandable that some will be deluded."

However, something quite remarkable happened two days ago. I was in my room writing. I knew a large gathering was taking pace in the large room on the upper floor. Suddenly I heard the most extraordinary outburst of voices, a kind of mingled singing, shouting, crying, laughing, even the sound of what seemed like dancing. After a few moments they burst out of the room and rushed outside. By this time others in the area had come to investigate. The leader of the community, a northerner named Peter, shouted for silence and then began to give an impassioned explanation for what was happening. As far as I could gather he was attributing the massive burst of excitement to his friend Jesus who had died but who somehow—he claimed—was alive.

I had gone out on the roof to see what was happening, only to find the master of the house there before me. He was gazing down as if he could not believe what he was seeing. I followed his gaze to see his wife and their son Mark, my student, in the crowd, both of them seemingly intoxicated with whatever madness had come over everybody. The master said nothing. I could see tears in his eyes as he turned to go down the steps into the house.

Do I know what to make of all this, my friend? Frankly I don't. In this country religious movements sweep by with almost depressing frequency. And yet, one thing about that crowd I was looking at stays with me. I began to notice that somehow, in spite of language barriers, a message was getting across that something of immense significance was taking place. Some sneered, but very few. I could see conversations beginning to take place as well as groups forming.

I felt I had seen enough. I retreated to my room and my writing.

While all of this was a few days ago, I still have a nagging question. Did I witness a pivotal moment, or is this merely a passing enthusiasm that has already claimed one death and may well claim others? I notice my student Mark is inattentive, as if his mind is elsewhere. His mother's certainly is. I find that I fear greatly for this good family.

Andronicus, it will be so good to taste the comparative calm and sanity of Athens once again.

Health and prosperity to you, old friend,
Gregory

CHAPTER 23

The Convert

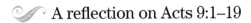 A reflection on Acts 9:1–19

Saul of Tarsus, a dangerous enemy of the emerging Christian movement, has been shocked and traumatized by his encounter with the risen Christ on the Damascus Road. He has been brought to a house in the city, presumably by his staff, who leave him there. He is blind, alone, and almost certainly fearful. He knows well there are many who have good cause to wish him harm. But to Saul's astonishment and relief, Ananias, a courageous member of the local Christian community, comes to him. The visit transforms Saul's relationship with the group.

We can assume that Saul, later choosing the name Paul, would never have forgotten this visit. While we have no record of his doing so, there must have been some occasion when Paul would have tried to communicate his gratitude. I have tried to imagine a letter that he might have written to express his thanks . . .

Antioch in Syria, 35 C.E.

To Ananias who visited me,

I had hoped to meet you in person, but I hear that you have left the city and no one in the community seems to know where you have gone. In the hope that I can find you, I have asked that this letter of mine be circulated among the many groups in the greater Antioch area, and even beyond in the province. I seek you, Ananias, for one reason—to thank you.

You cannot imagine the state of mind I was in by the time you reached out to me. I had lost my sight. Thank God it eventually returned, but at that particular time I did not know that it would. Everything I had ever believed in and worked for had been devastatingly challenged. I had been convinced that the teachings of your Jesus—now, thank God, also mine—were completely spurious and a serious threat to Judaism as I had always known and understood it. As you well know, and as I write again here to my shame, I had spent a number of years focusing all my energies on attacking the newly forming communities. In doing this I know now that I was attacking him.

If you ever get this letter you will be glad to know that I can see again, albeit with slightly less clarity than before. Ananias, I am quite convinced that my recovery began with your visit. I recall hearing footsteps. I had no idea who was coming or for what purpose. I knew well there were many in the city who had good cause to wish my death. I do recall a terrible sense of helplessness and fear.

You may not remember this, but you touched me. You then said two words that meant everything to one in my position. After all, I was alone, cut off from everything I had known, including a huge and powerful network where I had status, authority, and resources. All this I had lost in one stroke, until you came.

"Brother Saul," you said, your voice trembling with nervousness. In that moment you gave me welcome, fellowship, acceptance, community. But then you said something else that brought balm and order to my shattered universe. You said, "Brother Saul, the Lord Jesus Christ who met you on the way here has sent me . . . "

Ananias, if I needed of proof of the reality of what I had experienced on the Damascus Road, you gave it to me when you uttered the name of the one I now acknowledge as my Lord. Before that day, the name of Jesus served only to engender in me a deep and visceral hatred. Yet when you spoke his name I found myself reacting as I would to the naming of a dear friend. In that moment I knew beyond a shadow of a doubt that what had happened to me was totally real. I knew that he whom you named and the one who had addressed me on the road were one and the same person, offering me in the same moment both perfect freedom and freely accepted slavery. From now on I shall speak for and to him with deeds, with the energies of every moment of my life.

You gave me life, my friend, and in doing so you began the healing that eventually restored my sight. In another sense, you began the healing of my spirit that enabled me to see the new life being offered to me. Wherever you are Ananias, know that I, Paul, owe you my life in Christ, and for that gift given to me I owe you everything.

Your friend forever in Christ,
Saul, now Paul, his slave

CHAPTER 24

The Expatriate

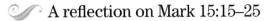 A reflection on Mark 15:15–25

Of the four gospels, three mention the experience of Simon of Cyrene. A mere bystander, he finds himself forced to carry the heavy crossbeam under which Jesus collapses as he is being taken to be crucified. We know nothing about Simon other than that he comes from the North African province of Cyrene. However, the fact that Mark, writing his gospel in Rome in 64 C.E., refers to Simon as "the father of Alexander and Rufus," suggests that the sons are by this time known in the Christian community. Again, when Paul is ending his letter to that same community by sending greetings to various people, he greets one named Rufus. All of which drew my mind to the possibility that forms this letter . . .

To Alexander and Rufus, beloved sons, and their families,

Springtime in Rome is so incredibly beautiful. Warms the bones of an old man. Why this letter now? Because I want to set down, for our beloved grandchildren, the event that changed all our lives, now thirty years ago. You two know it well but, as I said, it is for your children, Julia and Drusus, Agrippina and Simon.

I remember I turned forty that year; you were then eighteen and twenty-one. Two years earlier, we had nearly lost your mother. For some months I thought I would go out of my mind with worry. I was so grateful for her recovery that it spurred the idea of our making a pilgrimage together to Jerusalem.

We had left Palestine and settled in Cyrene, your grandfather's town. I had been born on that lovely Libyan coast. As you know, I met your mother there. Our family business was prospering. I knew that you boys were just old enough to stay behind and look after things for a couple of months. I booked passage for your mother and me on a galley that would call in at Alexandria before going up to Joppa on the coast of Palestine.

The voyage was uneventful, very pleasant in spring. Jerusalem was teeming with people for Passover, expatriates like ourselves everywhere. I always find a big city exciting. You boys must have inherited this from me because here we all are in Rome, you two in your own business, your old parents as your neighbors in our small villa.

It was early morning on our third day in Jerusalem. Thank God I had left your mother resting in our lodgings. I was strolling by shops on one of the narrow streets when there was a sudden disturbance. There were shouts, people backing away to each side. I caught a glimpse of a Roman helmet. As the center of things got closer I realized it was an execution detachment. When I saw the prisoner, I was shocked. He could barely walk. He had obviously been lashed within an inch of his life. The weight of the heavy crossbeam he was trying to carry was making his knees buckle every few paces. He happened to fall again just as he reached where I was standing.

To this day what happened then is a blur. I realized the centurion in charge was shouting at me. I heard "You! Yes you! Pick it up!" I was terrified. Fingering a whip, he strode toward me, pointed to the heavy beam and said very deliberately and menacingly, "Pick it up *now*!" Trembling, I was barely able to obey him.

We followed the street to the gate in the city wall, leaving most of the crowd behind, all except the hardened few who enjoy an execution. At the top of a low mound there was an appalling sight. Two crosses already held two others, both obviously in unspeakable agony. The centurion turned to me and barked, "You. That's enough. You can go." I turned to go, and then it happened. The prisoner turned toward me and mouthed a hoarse, "Thank you."

I didn't wait. I ran, down the slope, in under the city gate, along the streets, ran until I reached our lodgings. When your mother saw me, she was shocked. I think I burst into tears before throwing myself on the bed, exhausted, and slept.

You know the rest of this family story, how we returned home to Cyrene. I was still haunted by that "thank you" and by the eyes in that battered face. You remember how I tried for the next few years to find out something about the prisoner I had helped. Then a colleague told me one day there was a group he thought I might like to meet. He and his wife had offered their house.

That evening, your mother and I heard a name I had not known. I heard about the man whose cross I had carried. I heard the unbelievable news that had brought this group of friends together. Somehow I knew that life would never again be the same for us.

As you well know, a few years passed. You two became gifted businessmen, found your wives, brought your children into the world. Life in the empire changed and you decided to sell the business in Libya and move north to Rome. Imagine our joy when both of your wives became involved with the community here. By then it had a name— Christian. Then came our even greater joy when you both became part of its life. All because I happened to be standing where someone fell, totally exhausted and in terrible pain, someone whom all of us as a family now call Savior.

My dear Alexander and Rufus, you have both done well in Rome. You will leave your children a magnificent inheritance. One thing I ask. Keep this letter. Pass it on to them. What it speaks of is precious beyond all else. Remember always our greeting:

Jesus is Lord.

Your loving father, Simon

CHAPTER 25

The Slave Owner

A reflection on Philemon verses 8–21

At one stage of his ministry, Paul found himself faced with a complex and sensitive situation. A young slave named Onesimus had run away and had come to Paul for refuge. The estate he had left was owned by Philemon whom Paul himself had evangelized.

If captured, a fugitive slave could face death. In spite of this, Paul advises Onesimus to go back, carrying a letter commending him to Philemon as a fellow Christian and therefore as now more than a slave. It is a risk both men must have known, but Onesimus takes the letter and returns. We do not have any reply from Philemon. My hope is that something like the following might have reached Paul eventually . . .

To Paul, friend and mentor,

I apologize for causing you anxiety by not replying sooner. The reason was my absence from home on a business trip. I returned only yesterday and was given my accumulated mail this morning. In it I found your letter about Onesimus.

First let me apprise you of how things stand. I have been away for over three weeks. I have been told that one week ago, Onesimus returned to our household and surrendered himself to the guard at the gates of my estate. As is customary, he has been kept in custody awaiting my return. As you can well imagine, the matter is high on my list of priorities.

Let me assure you that Onesimus has been well treated in custody. I have drilled my guards that everyone in my household, no matter what the circumstances, is to be treated with respect for their inherent humanity. That does not mean that I hesitate to apply the full extent of the law if I deem it warranted.

Paul, you must be aware that this young man's decision to run away is punishable by death. What you may not as clearly realize is that your request that I pardon him places me in a very difficult position. Not only will it be interpreted by some as personal weakness, but it will also cause me to run the risk of being myself taken to law by my fellow estate owners, all of whom own slaves. They will see my action as a threat to the whole system, one which they naturally wish to preserve. What I share with you now arises out of certain matters to which you refer in your letter.

It is now three years since your first visit to my home. You will recall that you and I first met in the villa of Titus Vitellius, our local governor. A group of us had been invited to meet you. I did not then know that both Titus and his wife Priscilla had become devotees of the new faith of Jesus of Nazareth. Little did I know that this faith would speak powerfully to my own heart and mind, and would draw both my wife Apphia and myself into its fellowship.

Even less did I realize the consequences that would flow from this newly found faith. Above all I would learn the essential worth of every human life now that our Christ has taken our flesh and died for all. I have come to see this new valuation of human life as a radically transforming element in the faith you and I now share. Also significant is that Onesimus himself now shares in this fellowship because of the effect you have had on him.

Paul, I have made a decision that I know will please you. As I said before, I cannot ignore what Onesimus has done. To do so leaves me open to possible legal challenge. If I were to lose that challenge it would destroy me financially and personally, not to mention devastate my family and, of course, eventually bring about the death of Onesimus.

We begin then with the decision that he must be punished in some way. I have made discreet enquiries and I find that one thing the law allows me to do is to imprison him on my own estate. This I have already done. It allows me to order the conditions of his imprisonment and to set him to whatever tasks I choose during the period he remains prisoner.

Speaking of such possible duties, I know you will be pleased at an inspired suggestion made by Apphia when we discussed this plan. We have decided that one of Onesimus's first tasks will be to make as many copies as possible of your own letters to the various communities around the eastern empire. These will of course include the letter you wrote to the community in Ephesus and the magnificent letter you wrote to the community in Rome. It now remains only for you to send me any other letters of which you may have retained a copy. In this way you will be spared many hours of the tedious task of making copies. There are far more worthy uses for your time.

So, my dear friend, I trust this news brings you joy. My hope is that in the passing of time any interest in this incident will subside. If any neighboring colleague does ask troublesome questions, I have resources to make it to his advantage to desist. As well, we are not the only estate-owning household in this province to be expressing interest in what some of us are quietly referring to as the New Way.

I send greetings from the many faces and voices you have yet to meet in our household church as it steadily grows. We pray for your safety on your ceaseless travels. Most of all, we pray that you may find an opportunity to fulfill your wish to come among us once again.

In Christ,
Philemon

CHAPTER 26

The C.E.O. in Philippi

A reflection on Acts 16:6–15
and Philippians 2:1–11

*Philippi was a growing city at the terminus of the Via
Egnatia, a main east/west highway of the Roman Empire.
Paul, with his companions Timothy and Silas, had crossed
to Europe from Asia. Their success in forming a Christian
community was due to a group of women, led by an affluent business woman named Lydia.*

*Sometime later Paul is under house arrest, most likely
in Rome. He writes to Philippi what is perhaps the warm-
est and most affectionate of all his letters, sending it by
Timothy. It strikes me that it is at least possible that Timothy may have returned with a reply from Lydia, whose
faithfulness and courageous leadership had brought into
being a strong and growing church . . .*

Paul, dear friend and mentor in Christ,

You will be surprised to receive this letter but I thought
it a wonderful opportunity to write to you now that Timothy
is preparing to leave for his long return journey.

Thank you from all of us for your letter. I know that Timothy will have lots to tell you. The really good news he has for you is about the house churches that have sprung up.

What we are all distressed to hear is that you are under some kind of custody there in Rome. From what Timothy tells us it is a form of house arrest. We understand you can have visitors and, wonderful for us and for other new churches, you can write letters. I remember when you were in the local jail here. One of our local earth tremors damaged the jail and freed you. Remember how you reassured the jailor? Well, guess who now has a regular group meeting in his house? Yes indeed, your friend the jailor.

Timothy stayed in my home while he was here. It meant so much to me and to all of us in the church to have him with us. He and I have had long chats about the faith that has sprung up among us so wonderfully. I say this because I want you, dear friend, to be proud of what you began here in Philippi. So much has happened since that day only a few short years ago when you and I met that morning, both of us with our friends, you with Silas and Timothy, and I with Euodia and Synthiche. We three were sitting together chatting down by the river when you three came along. Little did I realize that morning that my life, and now the lives of so many here in our small city, would be transformed by the good news you brought us of the risen Christ.

By the way, our once small city is much bigger than you remember. The highway becomes busier every year and the river boats take much more cargo down to Neapolis for the voyage to Troas and then all over the Eastern Empire.

I tell you all this because it affects me directly. My agency for garments with our exclusive purple dye has grown immensely—again because of the highway. Can you believe it, I now send shipments along the Via Egnatia as far west as Thessalonica on the Adriatic coast? As well I have orders going down the Aegean for Greek customers. Do you know that I even have an agency there in Rome itself?

Telling you this reminds me of the moment, soon after we first met, when I told you what I did for a living. I told you how I had moved from Thyatira and I was in the purple dye and garment trade. You were quite alarmed for me. You thought I was trespassing on the imperial monopoly on purple dye. I had to assure you that our dye came from a totally different source and therefore was a lot more affordable. You may get some idea of our success when you receive the gift I'm sending you with Timothy for your work.

Paul, I am pleased about my success for one reason. It makes it possible for me to be very generous, not only to the wonderful work you are doing, but also to the network of house churches that is spreading in the city and surrounding countryside. This work has grown grown even since we sent you a gift with Epaphroditus.

Dear Epaphroditus. I am so terribly sorry to hear from Timothy that he is too ill to return to us. Please assure him of our prayers for him in all our churches.

Speaking of illness, Paul, please for all our sakes and for our risen Lord's sake, please take care of yourself. Timothy tells me you have plans to go as far as Spain. Again, please take care.

My secret hope is that you will come back through Philippi again. From what you say in your letter we seem to mean a great deal to you. I know from things you have said that for some reason the work here in and around Philippi has blossomed in ways it has not done in some other places. I thank God for this because we can then be a comfort and inspiration to you when you are struggling with the care of all those other churches. I thank God too that I have been able to play at least a small part in all this.

Something I nearly forgot. You remember my friends Euodia and Synthiche? They too found Christ and committed themselves to him. Soon afterward they both had groups meeting in their homes. Those circles have grown.

I mention them, because for some reason, Timothy has seen that their friendship is being tested by some disagreement. It may be about the different ways in which they see some of their previous ideas about the spiritual world being grafted into our new Christian faith. They both have very good minds and both had read quite widely before their conversion, unlike me. I'm afraid I'm the practical one of the group. But then all of us are needed for Christ, aren't we, each of us with our different gifts? We'll continue to work at this and I am sure we will resolve it.

One last thought. Thank you beyond words for that simply beautiful passage in your letter to us, the one where you write, "Let the same mind be in you that was also in Christ Jesus." Thank you for this and for everything.

Your friend forever in Christ,

Lydia

CHAPTER 27

The Physician

A reflection on Luke 1:1–4
and Acts 1:1–5

As an introduction to his gospel, Luke writes to a friend named Theophilus. He tells Theophilus that the book has been written for him so that he "may know the truth concerning the things about which you have been instructed." Sometime later when Luke has completed his second book—the Acts of the Apostles—he again directs it to Theophilus.

Luke's dedication of his completed books must have arisen out of an already established friendship. If so, it is most unlikely that this is the first time Luke has written to Theophilus.

I asked myself if there might have been another occasion for Luke to write to his friend. From personal experience I know that it sometimes takes a particular experience to spur one to begin writing. A likely spur for Luke might have been his receiving the news of Paul's death in Rome. If this were indeed the case, what is more natural

*than that Luke would write to tell his friend Theophilus of
his plan for the two books . . .*

Theophilus, fellow student in the faith,

I write to tell you that a letter from Rome has brought
sad news—more than sad—tragic, since the loss to our
movement is incalculable. Paul is dead. He was executed
on the order of Nero, that monstrous lunatic who passes for
an emperor these days.

It appears that Paul was caught up in a purge instigated
by Nero after there had been a fire in Rome. It provided an
ideal opportunity to pin the blame on the Christian community. I have not yet received a list of names but I gather
that many whom I got to know when staying in Rome to
help Paul have died. Some of them I had come to treasure
as dear friends.

With Paul's death, I have lost the longest friendship of
my life. We knew one another since university years in Tarsus. His name was Saul in those days. I was there trying to
decide if I wished to pursue medicine; Paul was typically
certain he would study Jewish law.

Friends such as yourself are aware of our parting for
some years, a painful parting. I remember well the day I
went to him and told him I had become attracted to the small
but growing Christian community in the university. Paul
was adamant in his determination to oppose it. He curtly
told me that our friendship had ended. I was devastated. I
didn't realize then that his opposition would eventually turn
into implacable and even murderous enmity.

We didn't meet for a decade. I would hear from time to time of what he was doing. Once, when we both happened to be in Jerusalem at the same time, I took the risk of asking to see him. I tried to reason with him but it was quite useless. You can imagine my horror and sadness when I learned later that he had actually hounded a young Christian leader named Stephen to his death.

Then out of the blue I received the unbelievable news that Saul had undergone a complete and astonishing change of heart. At first, I dismissed the news as wishful thinking on the part of Christian friends. Dreading the confrontation, I went to him again, but this time found a completely transformed person! Here was Saul, now insisting on being called Paul, claiming a direct experience of the presence of the risen Jesus, and expressing his determination to become the champion of the new movement. No wonder there were many who simply refused to believe the conversion was genuine.

Since then, Theophilus, as you can imagine, everything has changed. Paul joined the community here in Antioch. It wasn't easy and it did not happen overnight. As you can imagine, the community was deeply suspicious at first. After all it was only months since this man was the sworn enemy of everything they believed in and stood for.

But Paul won their trust. From there so much has become possible. His magnificent mind and his newfound passion gave us all a much larger vision of the significance of Jesus and what he could mean, even for the empire. It's astonishing what has been achieved. Little did they know what would take place when they commissioned Paul and Barnabas on that first journey. Christian communities, large and small, have sprung up in city after city—even in Rome itself. The whole thing is utterly amazing. Mysterious and mighty indeed are the ways of God.

Theophilus, it's time for me to share some personal news. You know that in recent years I have been taking time off to visit some of the early communities that formed around allegiance to Jesus. There is a large one in Jerusalem, actually more than one. There is one in Caesarea Maritima, another in Joppa, and so forth. I've had countless conversations and taken endless notes.

As you also know, there is a great deal being written. The two authors that have made the deepest impression are John Mark and someone who uses the name Matthew. I value their work and am certainly going to incorporate a lot of it in what I hope to create, but I think they lack something really important. They lack what will interest the world—in fact the many worlds—outside Judaism.

I think that is something I can accomplish. As you know, I've travelled extensively and for years I've been in daily contact with Greeks, Romans, Syrians, Egyptians, and so on. This is precisely why I have made a decision I am really excited about.

Think of this Theophilus—I'm going to write about Jesus as Lord! Yes, I'm going to try my hand at a book, especially about the three years of Jesus's public ministry. I've even got some notes about his childhood and youth. I'll use both Mark's and Matthew's material, but I know I can add a lot. And maybe what's also important is to tell the story of what has happened since Paul came on the scene. Think of those communities in so many of the great cities and towns of the empire, even Rome itself. Who could have imagined it only twenty years ago?

Mind you, it will take time and travel. I have not yet worked out whether all this will take one or two volumes. There will have to be many more conversations with people, many of them getting on in years. I will have to talk more to those who travelled with Paul, as I did for a while. I'll have to read again the letters we have from Paul. That means I have to get my hands on the letters that were not circulated generally.

Anyway, give me time and you will eventually receive a copy of what I write. I assure you it will be set out in good order to give you a clear picture of this wondrous experience you and I and all our generation have been privileged beyond measure to share in.

He is risen, Theophilus! I can hear you across the miles saying, "Thanks be to God!" Yes indeed, old friend. Thanks be to God. I greet you in the richness of our many years of friendship, and in the fellowship of our Lord Jesus.

Luke

The People on the Hill

A reflection on Luke 23:44–56

It was a little after three in the afternoon on the hilltop. It had been some time since the last of the crucified figures had stirred. At this point, the centurion in charge of the execution moved toward the small squad who had worked this shift with him. The time had come to carry out what was considered to be a small act of mercy. It would at least bring the obscene process to an end.

In the case of the middle prisoner, long experience of these executions told the centurion that he had been dead for some time. He signaled for the legs of the two others to be broken.

The centurion was well aware that this was not an ordinary criminal execution, in that it also involved an element of politics. So it's possible that at this stage he may have taken the opportunity to look around to see who had remained throughout the whole dreadful process. If so, he would first have become aware of a group of four, three of them women. He had noticed them there from the very

115

beginning, three women and a young man. They were preparing to go; at least the three younger people seemed to be trying to persuade the older woman to come away. It was obvious that she was exhausted almost to the point of collapse.

If the centurion had looked further down the slope, he would have seen a large group of women. If he had looked even further, something unusual might have sparked his interest. Standing together, aloof from all others, were two men who, at least by the quality of their dress and the confidence of their bearing, were in some way official.

Some distance apart from the pair, other men were moving about restlessly. They were obviously rural and rather unkempt. From his various periods of army service around the country, the centurion mentally pegged them as Galilean. The interesting thing he noticed was that, while they paced about restlessly, they seemed reluctant to gather as a group, as if they did not want to be noticed as such. He made a mental note to pass this observation on to his superior when he made his overall report on the day's executions.

He gave his men the signal to begin clearing the hill. At this point, one of the two official-looking spectators came toward him, handed him a document that gave formal authorization for the body of the prisoner on the middle cross to be claimed for cleansing and burial. The centurion offered his men to help, but the Jewish official said that others who had not yet left the hill would respond to his request for assistance. The centurion realized that the Galilean group he had noticed were already gathering. As he watched them, he could not help noting the care and tenderness with which they went about the task. Obviously this had been carefully planned.

The two officials gave directions, the Galilean men did the actual removal, then the women were called to the body, which they swiftly wrapped before returning it to be carried away.

The centurion looked again at the sheet giving permission from the procurator for all this to take place. He noticed that one of the Jewish officials had arranged for the body to be placed in a private tomb on his estate. By now, he and his men were alone on the hill. Glad that his day's duty was over, the centurion dismissed the men, walked to his waiting horse, and left to begin writing his report while it was still vivid in his mind.

What the centurion would not report, because he was not even dimly aware of it, was that, while he had most certainly witnessed a death, he had also witnessed the birth of something that would in a comparatively short time not only affect the vast empire he served, but also spread to lands and peoples of whom neither he nor any other living person at that time was even aware. He had been present at the birth of the Christian faith.

When we, as inheritors of a two-thousand-year-old Christian tradition, consider that scene, we can see that even in the very first hours after Jesus's death, before anyone is thinking of resurrection as anything other than a desperate hope, a community of believers has already emerged. Why is this important?

Over the two thousand years since that long-ago day on a faraway hill, we Christians have tried to pierce the mystery we call resurrection. We continue that effort today. As we do, we can easily miss the fact that whatever it means to say that Jesus rose from the tomb, something else also rose from those events, something we can instantly and clearly understand.

That something is who we are, the Christian community. We are the people on the hill.

Acknowledgments

There are so many to whom I am thankful, but one must choose. To George Barter, my childhood ear specialist who, in a long-ago Ireland of very limited medical resources, when painful procedures were unavoidable, comforted a small boy with the gift of a new book at every appointment. To Peter, rabbi and teacher, who opened to me the vast and wonderful world of midrash. To Richard LeSueur, cherished colleague, who first generously shared with me his extensive and intimate knowledge of the land where the events of our Lord's life unfolded when we taught together at St. George's College, Jerusalem, in 1993. To Helen Barron, longtime friend, who encouraged me to consider the possibility of publication. To my editor Sharon Pearson, who welcomed me warmly into her stable of writers. Finally, to Ian Alexander, dear friend, who encouraged and guided me toward completing the work.

Scripture Index